Tonality and Musical Structure

TONALITY AND MUSICAL STRUCTURE

GRAHAM GEORGE

PRAEGER PUBLISHERS
New York · Washington

BOOKS THAT MATTER

Published in the United States of America in 1970
by Praeger Publishers, Inc., 111 Fourth Avenue,
New York, N.Y. 10003

Library of Congress Catalog Card Number: 72-109472

Printed in Great Britain

to
TJOT

ACKNOWLEDGMENTS

A book that takes some fifteen years to prepare has inevitably had much help from many sources, and I am glad to acknowledge it where I can.

I am grateful first to my students at Queen's University who, believing that they were concerned with something real, have often worked strenuously to help solve particular problems. To name them would be invidious, but I think of the student of engineering (taking a course in music to the astonishment of his colleagues) who pointed the way towards the concept called in this book 'opposition of tonal relation'. The concept was first expressed as a 'counterpoise' of tonalities. This student said, 'Under certain circumstances' (which he specified) 'I can hear what you mean by counterpoise. But under other circumstances' (which he specified) 'I can't'. He was, as further work made clear, quite right.

I think also of the three students in a seminar course on Romanticism, who responded with alacrity and devotion to the scandalous suggestion: 'Would you like to abandon the prescribed course and find out what Wagner really did?'; and the student who, filled with doubt about the theory of interlocking structures in dramatic music, convinced himself of its validity by attacking the *St Matthew Passion*, in which he expected it not to work; producing the observation, which appears on page 44 as if it were my own, concerning the relation of the tonal structure of that work to an aspect of its narrative structure.

I am grateful also to three colleagues on the staff of Queen's University who read the whole of the typescript: Dr F. R. C. Clarke, musician, and Drs Jon Wheatley, now of the University of California at Santa Barbara, and E. J. Bond, philosophers. Their criticisms have improved the book while leaving them free of responsibility for its content. To Dr Wheatley in particular I owe much for both formal and informal discussions of twentieth-century philosophy over a considerable period. His talent for finding holes in arguments has contributed greatly to making the book's theses linguistically manageable.

My four sons have with reasonable grace learnt to live with the abstracted air and the 'Not just now', and for that I thank them. All the phrases by which an author can thank his wife have been so used and used again as to have quite lost their expressive force. So I am reduced to the trite observations that mine has been certain when it seemed that no-one else was; a tower of strength in times of trouble; and an incomparable companion in times of joy. This is, I take it, sufficient reason to dedicate the book to her, even though the analysis of music is far from her deepest love.

A good deal of Part I appeared as an article, 'Tonality in the Structure of Dramatic Music 1607–1909', in *The Musical Quarterly*, vol. LII, no. 4, October 1966. My thanks are due to its editors for their permission to reprint the material in its original context.

An author getting a first book into print is adrift on an unknown sea, and his gratitude to an efficient editorial staff must be immense. Mine is at least that to Donald Mitchell, whose connection with the book, though (as far as I know) fittingly occasional and brief, has been decisive; to Alan Walker, of the BBC's Music Division, who fulfilled his duties as consultant editor with good-humoured skill and a relentless determination that the book should make the best of itself; and above all to John M. Thomson. Of him it would be epigrammatic to say that his unrelaxed vigilance relaxes every tension, but in fact his vigilance is such that there is never any tension to relax.

To make a book is something. But to make good friends among those who are making it is something extra.

GRAHAM GEORGE

Queen's University
Kingston, Ontario
1968

CONTENTS

PREFACE

In analysing music we have to do two things: first, search diligently until we find the closest possible description of what
happens in the music; then search diligently until we have found
means to express an acceptable structural interpretation of the
musical happenings. Although it need never occur that we cannot describe the happenings as far as they need description for
the purpose of analysis, it may quite often occur, especially in
large-scale works, that we cannot so master the material as to
give both a clear statement of the overall structure and the relation of each part to the whole. In such a case the discipline
of having learnt to say clearly what we mean in small matters
will have guided us to the recognition of our insufficiency, tem-
porary or permanent, in large ones; will save us from the need
of hiding behind verbal smoke-screens, however venerable; and
will enable us to say with steadfast dignity and decreasing surprise: 'I don't know'.

What follows is an attempt to attack some very well-known
problems in structural analysis with only two prejudices: against
muddle-headedness and against dishonesty. It is addressed to
two sorts of people, in overlapping categories: professional
musicians of all sorts, and that fabulous, many-headed, sometimes gullible but often tough-minded creature the 'intelligent
layman'. I do not pretend that the latter will find it easy reading.
But its basic assertions concern him directly and are not so
technical as to be beyond understanding. The layman will find
here some real answers to real questions and, at any rate in
matters of fact, no unreality at all.

We are concerned in this book with certain aspects of musical
structure, approached as consciously apprehensible phenomena.

Thus we are not concerned with the theory of thematic unification initiated by Schoenberg and developed by Rudolph Réti, Hans Keller, Alan Walker and others. This theory defines a masterpiece as a work of art all of whose thematic contrasts vary a basic musical idea, of which neither the composer nor the listener need—or indeed for the most part can—be conscious. The theory is worthy of respect as well as criticism, but it cannot answer questions to which it does not apply.

The book divides itself into three parts, the first being a hypothesis, based on a series of statements of fact, about the characteristic structures of Baroque, Classical and Romantic dramatic works: operas, oratorios and settings of the Passion texts. In this part, although I believe the hypothesis to be valid and have supported it with evidence, there are many works still to be analysed before we can be sure that the process of locating the relevant factors is reasonably complete. Even within the works already analysed and shown to conform to the hypothesis there are plenty of details—as might be expected in such large and complex works—on which differing points of view can have full play without invalidating the hypothesis. Further, some readers may wish to deny validity to the hypothesis; and if they can support their denial with facts we shall have made a notable advance. For the act of denial will demand the formulation of a stronger hypothesis where until now we have had none at all.

The second part of the book consists of a series of statements about the tonal procedures characteristic of Baroque, Classical and Romantic instrumental music. Here, since the structures are all relatively small, it may not be arrogant to claim a fair proportion of completeness, except in the sense that as many examples could be adduced as there are pieces of music in the areas concerned.

The third part considers the principle of progressive tonality as exemplified in the music of Mahler, Hindemith, Mozart and Nielsen.

My purpose throughout the book is not to reiterate what has been adequately stated before, but to confine the discussion to those musical structures in which tonality is of paramount importance and to stress the tonal aspect. This restriction of purpose has the advantage that it takes into account all the most important procedures of the periods under discussion, and leaves out everything of secondary interest. Thus in the Baroque period the discussion centres on the fugue, the concerto and the rondeau—all structures whose nature has been often misrepresented by an undue analytical attachment to thematic factors and neglect of tonal ones. In the Classical period, instrumental music is represented in the discussion primarily by sonata-form. Almost as important is the concerto first-movement structure; and much less important in this period, but still important enough to be discussed, are the rondo and the fugue.

All that I have to say will presuppose (i) that a work of art is a meaningful unit as distinct from a mere succession of events; and (ii) that the comprehension of a series of musical procedures—the gathering of them up into a meaningful unit—requires a unifying mental act.

This 'unifying mental act' is nothing strange to our normal modes of thought; it is the procedure by which we pull the individual members of any perceived group *into* a group. We recognise numbers of people in civilian clothes as a group of civilians if there is nothing further to distinguish them; as people waiting for a bus, or an opportunity to buy, if they have formed a queue; as soldiers if they are recognisably uniformed as such. Not only homogeneous objects but also heterogeneous ones seen together may be recognised as a group if they relate to a common context. Even a jumble of odds and ends is unified into 'a jumble' by this characteristic tendency of our minds to unify our experiences.

Thus music has the choice of being regarded as a jumble—and it is probably not too cynical to suppose that many people listen to it in this character, however agreeable a jumble it may be—or as a structure, comprehensible because the composer made it so, in more sophisticated terms.

The first of these presuppositions—that a work of art is a

meaningful unit—implies among other things that its overall structure must be capable of expression in a few terms, for we are not capable of recognising as a single unit a structure expressed in a large number of terms.

The second presupposition—that the comprehension of a series of musical procedures requires a unifying mental act—implies that this unifying act must operate on either thematic or tonal procedures. For neither rhythm, despite its being implicit in everything else that happens in music, nor harmony except under special conditions of very limited application, has the capacity to provide the basis for it. Traditional analysis appears to have assumed, or to have allowed itself to be hypnotised by its own discussions into believing, that thematic procedures are capable of providing its basis. But one only has to see in one's mind's eye the thematic analysis of a complex fugue or a Wagnerian music-drama to recognise that there is no basis here for a unifying mental act because there is no way of reducing the mass of materials to the comprehensibility of a few terms. The reason for this is that reduction of a complex mass of material to a few terms is nothing but a matter of grouping the complexities into areas bounded by materials acceptable as reiterations of each other. In complex works, thematic materials will not fulfil this function because either the same materials will occur in situations in which they cannot define the structure (for example, in a fugue or other ritornello structure where a large number of reiterations of the same materials occur), or they will occur in situations where, if they were to be regarded as fulfilling a boundary function, they would fulfil it in the wrong direction—which in fact they do not do. Such a situation would occur in the standard use of the opening material of a movement in sonata-form to indicate the return of the first tonality. Its purpose there is to act not as the end of something that began at the beginning, but as a repetition, with an altered significance, of the beginning *as* a beginning. Tonalities, on the other hand, do have the capacity to act as boundary materials for the definition of a structure. They have it because each of them has implicitly the nature of a thought continuum, and so can be in a sense 'there' even when it is not there. So that the return 'home' in a tonal structure is not a refashioning of something 'like' what was there before (as a return to a thematic procedure is bound to be) but a return to something that has been there—and been 'home', even when it was out of sight—all the time.

In addition, the definition of structure by means of tonality creates the conditions for unlimited melodic and rhythmic freedom, and for harmonic freedom within the capacity of the chordal relations concerned to express the required tonalities. It is a matter of experience that, if we understand the tonal outline of even the most complex musical work—as long as it is a work of art, not a mere agglomeration of materials—that work will take on a life as it were of its own, in which it can provide its own explanations of its own procedures, its own functions, even its own purposes. Music, that is to say, has its own logic which, though untranslatable, is nevertheless communicable.

INTRODUCTION

We are concerned for the most part with musical structure
during the three hundred years in which western music was
dominated by the functions of major-minor tonality, and my
argument assumes audible and consciously definable relationships between keys—what Tovey, in his *Beethoven*, called 'a
verifiable musical experience'.

If the reader and I are to understand each other we must
first reach agreement that keys *are* related in audible and consciously definable ways.

TONALITY AND THE LISTENER

We should agree, I think, that there is no way of apprehending
music except by hearing. Even the famous 'sitting in my easy-
chair, score on knee, getting more satisfaction than from any
performance' involves an imaginative 'hearing' of what the
notation stands for. Thus, in music, a change is only a change
insofar as it can be heard: an imperceptible change of key is a
contradiction in musical terms. If a change of key is something
which can be felt, and if it is felt as an 'away'-ness and if there
is more than one such away-ness, it must also be felt as a change
in one direction as distinct from another. And in the nature
both of sensation and of the concept of direction, both the
sensation and the direction must be describable, though not
necessarily very accurately and not necessarily in the same terms
for everyone.

There is, we know, some difference of opinion about the best
terminology for these descriptions, but two important factors
are not in question. First, that there are such sensations.
Second, that whatever terminology individual disputants may
prefer, the sensations created by the same musical materials in

listeners reasonably advanced in musical experience (setting aside such subjective experiences of relationship as absolute significance of particular keys and inter-relationships of musical and non-musical experiences) are effectively the same. If the sensation produced by a change of key in the direction x is to be described as y, then a further change in the direction x will produce a further sensation describable as some sort of y. If this is not so then the materials of music are entirely unreliable and no composer can know what will be the effect on anybody (including himself, when he hears it performed) of what he writes.

Tovey's names for the sensation of going on to the sharp side and the flat side of a given key were, respectively, 'bright' and 'dark'. With some modification I shall continue to use these

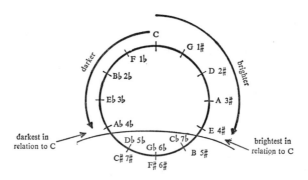

terms, having been unable to find any better. We shall recognise an increasing 'brightness' of sensation as we move through four major keys of the 'circle of fifths' on the sharp side of any starting key, and 'bright' as describing also the sensation of any major key in relation to any minor; an increasing 'darkness' of sensation as we move through four major keys of the circle on the flat side of any starting key, and 'dark' as describing also the sensation of any minor key in relation to any major.

(The sixth key of the circle, in either direction—being in equal temperament the same key, enharmonically different in notation—is totally ambiguous in relation to the starting key, and the fifth key in each direction partakes in a lesser degree of the same relative ambiguity.)

DIAGRAMMATIC SYMBOLS USED IN THE BOOK

To enable the eye to survey considerable areas of music at a glance, movements will be structurally diagrammed by means of letter-names and superior and inferior figures.

Letter-names will represent aurally determinable sections of music: sections concerning which, in listening to the music, one can say 'That's *that*'. The size of such sections will depend on the degree of refinement required in the analysis, bearing in mind that 'refinement' in this sense cannot apply to the overall analysis of a structure, but only to its internal details.

The relative size of sections indicated by letter-names is roughly indicated by the use of capitals or small letters. The use of the same letter in both forms indicates thematic relationship between the two, the smaller being a reference to the larger.

A variant of a theme is indicated by a superior figure associated with the letter-name. The difference between a 'reference' to a theme and a 'variant' of it is that the reference is certainly smaller than the theme and may be fragmentary, whereas the variant constitutes a new presentation of effectively the same theme. Thus:

Theme	indicated by A
Reference to that theme	indicated by a
Variant of that theme	indicated by A^1
Variant of the reference	indicated by a^1

The *key* of the material represented by a letter-name is indicated by an inferior figure drawn from the scheme, arbitrary and convenient, shown below.

The keys most frequently requiring reference are referred to by the Arabic numerals 1 to 4, and these same numerals are used to signify in addition corresponding general relationships. The double use of the symbols is justified by the fact that any key in relation to any other key has a specific relationship (e.g., that of being its dominant or its subdominant), and also a general relationship, in the sense of Tovey's 'bright' or 'dark' (e.g., the dominant is also *bright* in relation to the tonic; the subdominant is *dark* in relation to it. Thus:

Inferior figures used in the general *sense mean:*	*Inferior figures used in* the specific *sense mean:*
Home	1 Tonic
Bright	2 Dominant
Brighter	3 Dominant of the dominant
Dark	4 Subdominant

The 'general' sense of the symbols is always used in the case of overall structures, the 'specific' sense being reserved for more detailed analyses.

The following abbreviations, though they are probably self-explanatory, are perhaps worth listing:

Chromatic material	chrom
Extension or extended	ext
Modulating or modulation	mod
Chord	ch
Dominant	dom
Sequence (or sequential)	seq
Suspense	susp
Orchestral statement of themes	OST
Section of opposite tonal relation	SOTR
Relative major	rel ma
Relative minor	rel mi
Supertonic $\frac{\text{major}}{\text{minor}}$	$\text{II}^{\text{ma}}_{\text{mi}}$
Mediant $\frac{\text{major}}{\text{minor}}$	$\text{III}^{\text{ma}}_{\text{mi}}$
Submediant $\frac{\text{major}}{\text{minor}}$	$\text{VI}^{\text{ma}}_{\text{mi}}$

Thus, for example, the first twelve bars of the first Brandenburg Concerto are expressed on page 123 as:

$$A_1 \quad B_1 \quad a_1 \quad b_1 \quad a^1_{seq} \quad b^1_{seq} \quad ext_1 \quad C_1$$

meaning that the movement starts with thematic material dominated by a tune or counterpoint of tunes, and that that material is followed by new thematic material. There follows a reference to A and a reference to B, and these references reappear sequentially—a procedure requiring diagrammatic representation by means of 'variant' signs on both the thematic fragments a and b. All of this is in the tonic key, and we are not concerned from a structural point of view whether the sequential process involves change of key or not.

The second line of the diagram of this movement appears as:

$$\text{on } A_{1-2} \quad \text{on } B_{II \; mi-rel \; mi-1} \quad \text{on } C_4$$

meaning that material based on theme A moves from the tonic to the dominant, after which material based on theme B appears in the supertonic minor and modulates through the relative minor to the tonic and is followed by material based on theme C, in the subdominant.

PART I

A Theory of Interlocking Structures

PART I

A Theory of Interlocking Structures

Schoenberg, in an essay in *Style and Idea*, says: '. . . I refuse to believe that in the great masterworks [of opera] pieces are connected only by the superficial coherence of the dramatic proceedings . . . something must have satisfied the master's sense of form and logic. We may not be able to discover it, but certainly it exists.'*

Analysts have for the most part maintained an oracular silence about musical structure in large-scale dramatic works written to a text. Since it is tonality which provides, if not an exclusive, at any rate an important answer to the question, we can understand that the twentieth-century master who first advocated the entire abandonment of tonality would not be the one to break that silence. The narrative is, as he saw, a structural factor. But clearly it cannot be the musical one, and it is presumably the musical structure to which he refers, since 'the master' whose sense of form and logic is to be satisfied is the composer.

When we say—what most people would be prepared to grant —that the musical structure is related to the narrative we have already implied the existence of a musical structure. But that structure has never yet been defined, though partial attempts have been made.

In an article in the *Zeitschrift für Musikwissenschaft* (III (1920– 1921), 518–34) entitled 'Händels Oper "Rodelinde" und ihre neue Göttinger Bühnenfassung' Rudolf Steglich hypothesises a combined tonal and narrative-psychological structure which he

* Philosophical Library, p. 143.

extends not only to all Handelian but all Baroque opera. By considering musical and narrative aspects of structure in combination he establishes certain symmetries in individual scenes and acts in *Rodelinde*. Through the four scenes constituting Acts I and II the method works well, but problems appear in Act III. There, in order to bring the internal relations of the act, as well as its relation to the rest of the opera, into conformity with his thesis, he is forced into a degree of argumentative subtlety bordering on evasiveness. Nevertheless Steglich's work is impressive and deserves renewed study. Its weakness lies in its failure to establish a purely musical structure before attempting to define a structure combining both musical and narrative factors.

Hugo Leichtentritt, in his *Händel* (1924), starts out as if he is going to forestall the present argument. He says, after paying tribute to Steglich: 'Handelian opera is derived throughout from musical-architectonic laws. It is first and foremost music . . .' (p. 598). 'We must rediscover . . . what an important artistic factor tonality is in Handel: what powerful, wide-ranging structures were made possible for him through an understanding of the potentialities of tonal relationships. The individual parts of an act are often devised in a subtle, ingenious, and structurally significant relationship of tonalities and successions of tonalities' (p. 600 et seq.), and he gives on page 643 a tonal analysis of Act I of *Amadigi* in Steglich's manner. But in the end it becomes clear, when he says that [Handelian opera's] 'main theme, its basic problem, is a conflict of emotions', that his own interest lies in Handel's use of tonality for the expression of specific meaning—a narrative, not a main musical-structure factor. He shows, for example, the tonal relation between the world-of-magic music and the world-of-reality music in Act I of *Orlando*.

The hypothesis I wish to put forward asserts that the structure of large-scale musical works in the major-minor period, whether or not composed to a text, is *essentially* tonal, and that, where such a work ends in a key other than that in which it began, it consists of two closed tonal structures interlocking.

The concept of a musical structure ending in a key other than that in which it began is applied in western instrumental music only in and after the period of 'break-up' of major-minor tonality, at the end of the nineteenth century. In dramatic music, on the other hand—in opera, oratorio and Passion music—it was applied almost from the beginning of the Baroque. For this reason, as well as because the hypothesis itself emerged from an investigation of the structure of opera, I shall present the case for it first in terms of dramatic music, following it with a brief consideration of the application of the principle in instrumental music of the late nineteenth century and the early twentieth, referring particularly to the music of Mahler, Nielsen, Richard Strauss and Hindemith.

TYPES OF STRUCTURE

In the history of opera from Monteverdi to Wagner, there are two main types of tonal structure: the 'closed' structure, which begins and ends in the same key and thereby provides comprehensibility of overall structure at once; and what we shall call the 'interlocking' structure, in which two 'closed' structures on different tonal centres overlap so that the total structure ends in a key other than that in which it began. It is presumably this type which has led generations of musicians to suppose that, where it occurs, there is no comprehensible tonal structure at all. Before entering on the main discussion of such cases, the reader must be satisfied, by reference to smaller-scale examples, that such a structure is musically (audibly) comprehensible.

Whatever is here put forward as a solution to a structural problem is a musical procedure which can be *heard* in one of two ways: either in the normal process of aesthetic apprehension, or by a special act of attention. Whatever cannot be heard by one or other of these means is irrelevant to our purpose.

The assumption on which we work is that a composer designs his music as sounds to be heard, not merely in his own or anyone else's head, but by the normal process of receiving 'real' sounds through the ear. This being so, the procedures embodied in these sounds must be comprehensible ones, and there is no way of 'comprehending' musical procedures—the very word 'comprehending' being used here only in an analogous sense—except by hearing them and recognising their interrelated functions. For the composer, this act of comprehension is the starting point, for the listener it is the finishing point: for the composer, it is that from which the sound to be heard by the listener springs; for the listener (even when he is the composer), it is that which the sound can bring about when it reaches the mind that wants to understand. For there are the two ways in which men's minds want to 'understand' works of art: the first and primal, by the path of sensitive aesthetic apprehension; the second and cerebral, by the path of analysis. This latter has many side-tracks leading nowhere, and the only way of avoiding them is to make sure, through the test of audibility, that the path of analysis and the path of aesthetic apprehension are going the same way.

The history of musical analysis is littered with discussions of pseudo-structures existing only in the minds of their theorist inventors. We need mention only the traditional exegesis of classical sonata-form on the one hand and the mountainous mirage—based, like a mirage, on reality—of Alfred Lorenz's imagining in his books on Wagner's music-drama. As to the former we need only observe, anticipating a later chapter, that as a generalisation (and it is difficult to imagine what other function it can have) it excludes most of Haydn and Beethoven and fails to mention many of the most interesting things about Mozart. As to the latter, it would seem that an analysis of *Tristan und Isolde* which describes as being in E minor a work in which everything of structural importance happens in C, A flat and B major can only be based on ingenious manipulation of diagrams, not on the sound of the music.

We are dealing here with consciously apprehensible elements of musical structure. Thus one of the chief tests of the validity of its analysis must be that, when one thinks back on the work concerned, the important elements of the analysis coincide with what come back to mind as the most important elements of the work. The significance to the analyst of this test cannot be overestimated.

I shall exhibit two simple examples of interlocking structure to demonstrate that such things exist. The first, Sachs' tutoring of Walther in Act III of *Die Meistersinger*, is relatively small in scale. The second, the overall structure of Haydn's *Creation*, is larger but equally clear-cut.

Sachs and Walther begin their conversation in a very firmly announced E flat major which in due course moves to and establishes its dominant, returning at Sachs' 'Sind Freunde beid', steh'n gern sich bei' to a firm cadence in E flat. The first two verses of the song are then composed in C major, and, when Walther loses patience, the scene ends with a sudden return to and a considerable extent of E flat, very decisively established. So far we have a large-scale E flat structure (though short relative to the length of the opera) with C major as a very bright subordinate key contained in it. Beckmesser's petty larceny follows in D (minor to major) alternating with an E flat whose purpose may well be to keep what turns out to be an interruption from straying too far from the main tonalities. Then Sachs and Eva talk, ostensibly about where the shoe pinches, in A flat, Walther appears in the door in pure-love's B major and the third verse of the song returns in C. Beckmesser's D, one-kind-of-love's A flat, and the purest ecstasy of love's B major are explained below (p. 62) in relation to other parts of the whole structure; but there is no doubt at all that, when Walther sings his same tune in the same tonality of C, the listener's mind goes homing to the first two verses, of which this third is the structural conclusion. A moment ago we had C major as a subordinate key in an E flat structure. Now it is a structure of its own with E flat as the subordinate key. And in fact the mind not merely accepts but insists upon the true description of its sensation as two interlocking structures, neither of which can be said to be subordinate to the other.

Haydn's *Creation* puts its opening 'Representation of Chaos' in a clear, however chromatically ornamented, key of C minor and the tonality of C is structurally important from the beginning of the work through 'The Heavens are Telling' to the duet of Adam and Eve and the ensuing large-scale chorus at the beginning of Part III. But the work ends in B flat, and the other

Haydn—*The Creation*

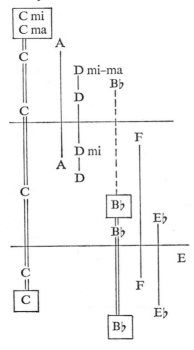

Representation of Chaos
'Let there be light'
'Now vanish before the holy beams'
'The marvellous work'
'Rolling in foaming billows'
'With verdure clad'
'Awake the harp'
'The heavens are telling'

'On mighty pens'
'Be fruitful all'
'Most beautiful'
'Now heaven in fullest glory'
'In native worth'
'Achieved is the glorious work'
'On Thee each living soul awaits'
'Achieved is the glorious work'

'In rosy mantle'
'By thee with bliss'
'O Star, the fairest pledge of day'
'Hail, bounteous Lord'
'Graceful consort'
'Praise the Lord'

pillar of this interlocking structure of B flat is found in the two lively choruses 'Achieved is the glorious work', which constitute, together with their E flat middle section (the duet of Gabriel and Uriel) the end of Part II.

D. F. Tovey tripped and fell over this with a crash appropriate to the size of his gifts. For he seriously announces, in Volume V of the *Essays in Musical Analysis*, that when he performs *The Creation* he always stops it at the Adam-and-Eve duet because that brings it to a close in the key in which it began, and because he doesn't want—now—to hear about our first ancestors' connubial bliss, though he would like to hear the music another time. An aberration truly worthy of his genius! For either a great composer 'knows' what he is doing, or he doesn't: where 'knows' refers to the artist's certainty that he has 'got it right', or as right as it's ever going to be, and where 'what he is doing' refers to the provision of music's untranslatable yet communicable logic. When Tovey decided to redesign *The Creation* he asserted among other things that he, Tovey, knew more about the necessary structure of that work than its composer did. And since Tovey makes his admiration of Haydn's structural abilities abundantly clear, in doing so he flew in the face not only of his own opinion of Haydn but also of his whole concept of classical structure so far as one can deduce it from the sum of his writings. *The Creation* is an interlocking structure consisting of C and B flat, and it has it in common with *Tristan und Isolde*, another large-scale interlocking structure, that the second main tonality first occurs at the end of the second of three parts, to recur at the end of the third.

So much for preliminaries. Discussion of a series of operas and religious works from Monteverdi to Bach and Handel will indicate how this and other tonal patterns are put into effect.

BAROQUE DRAMATIC STRUCTURES

Monteverdi's *Orfeo*, written in 1607, is the first opera by a composer of the front rank. It is more modal than truly major or minor; but with this proviso, and despite the high proportion of G minor and major in Acts III, IV and V, it is a closed structure in D minor. It could indeed be argued that it was not Monteverdi's intention to end the work with the brief and tonally rather indeterminate instrumental *moresca* in D (modal) minor, but that the second verse of the preceding G (modal) major chorus was to be sung after it. From a structural point of view, the decision is of slight importance. An ending in G would be more than justified by the amount of that tonality in the last three acts, and the overall structure would then be D and G interlocking, with the G structure starting immediately after the prologue with the first chorus of Act I. Whichever solution is chosen, to deny pride of structural place to tonality in this work would be to assume Monteverdi capable of writing almost the whole of an opera on the tonal centres of D and G without being aware of it.

The C major toccata with which the work opens forms the first element of a procedure frequently used in dramatic works: a 'subsidiary tonal thread'. (I shall leave aside the question of the transposition of the toccata to D major if the trumpets are muted, since it is not of major structural significance.) C major runs through the first part of the work without assuming major structural importance, and it also exemplifies another frequent tendency in writers of dramatic music: that of beginning a work in a tonality other than that or those which are to be its mainstays. Handel, for example, begins *Messiah* in E minor-to-major and uses that tonality as a subsidiary tonal thread; the main tonality of the work, after a dominant preparation at the chorus 'And the glory of the Lord', being D (minor-to-major) starting with the bass recitative 'Thus saith the Lord'. In the same composer's opera *Sosarme* there is a refinement of the process of beginning with a tonality other than a main one. The key of A with which it opens is consistently associated with the key of D (twice as A major, once as A minor) until the end of Act II (which is an A minor-to-major act). After that, D makes its final appearance shorn of A to complete the first element of an interlocking D/F structure.

Starting with the D minor prologue which follows on the toccata, *Orfeo* passes from an interlocking D minor/G minor in Act I through a continuation of that interlocking process in Act II. Act II, taken as a separate unit, is a G minor-to-major structure with a dark middle: this time Charon's F major (dark in relation to G major, which has preceded it), and the main

thread of D minor. (Whether Charon's F is psychologically
related to the messenger's F in Act II is a matter of interest but
not of immediate relevance.) The fourth act is a G minor structure with nothing but the subsidiary thread of C in the middle,

Monteverdi—*Orfeo*

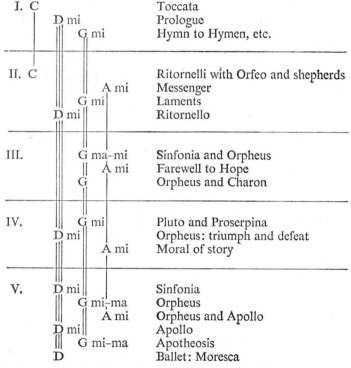

I. C			Toccata
	D mi		Prologue
		G mi	Hymn to Hymen, etc.
II. C			Ritornelli with Orfeo and shepherds
		A mi	Messenger
	G mi		Laments
	D mi		Ritornello
III.		G ma–mi	Sinfonia and Orpheus
		A mi	Farewell to Hope
		G	Orpheus and Charon
IV.	G mi		Pluto and Proserpina
	D mi		Orpheus: triumph and defeat
		A mi	Moral of story
V.	D mi		Sinfonia
		G mi–ma	Orpheus
		A mi	Orpheus and Apollo
	D mi		Apollo
	G mi–ma		Apotheosis
	D		Ballet: Moresca

(Indications of relation between tonality and text in this outline diagram
are more generalised than those in more detailed diagrams. They refer to
areas rather than to one-to-one relationships.)

followed by D minor; and the fifth act is G minor–major
throughout, until the return of D minor in the *moresca*.

In this opera the key of A minor is reserved chiefly for the
'Ahi, caso acerbo' of the second-act announcement of Eurydice's
death, and for the moment at the end of Act IV when Orfeo
loses her for the second time: a use of tonality for 'specific

meaning' comparable to, but not as strongly developed as, Wagner's subjective tonal procedures.

With Lully's *Amadis*, modality being now out of the way but for vestiges, we enter upon the more complex relationships between the parts of an opera which characterise the remaining history of opera until the dissipation of major–minor tonality into the functions of the twelve-note scale. *Amadis* is an interlocking structure G (minor-to-major)/C (minor-to-major) in which the C structure, although foreshadowed at the end of the first act, becomes a main structural function at the beginning of the third. Within this outline there are clearly marked structures.

The overall structure of Purcell's *Dido and Aeneas* (see page 38), though it is clearly tonal, conforms to no other pattern in general use by dramatic writers either in the Baroque period or later. With the exception of the little E minor chorus 'Cupid only throws the dart', the whole of Scene 1 is in C minor-to-major, which thereafter does not return. Except for the witches' duet, the whole of Scene 2 is in F minor-to-major, which thereafter does not return. Except for Aeneas' recitative, the whole of Act II is in D minor-to-major, which thereafter does not return. (D minor had been the key of the witches' duet.) Act III is divided about equally between B flat and G minor.

As it stands, we can note the following tonal facts about it. (1) There is a strong similarity of structure between the first, second and third scenes, and particularly the first two: both moving from a tonic minor to its major, the same tonal centre accounting for the whole act except for one brief area. (2) From Scene 2 of Act I to the end of the 'groves' scene in Act II (that is, nearly to the end of the act), the tonal movement is from F to its relative minor twice. (3) This duplicated procedure is answered in Act III by movement from B flat to its relative minor (twice if you count the brief element of B flat at the beginning of 'Great minds against themselves conspire').

No other dramatic work whether Baroque, Classical or Romantic has, in my experience, failed to yield up a compre-

Lully—*Amadis*

G mi–ma–mi   Overture–Prologue–Overture
G mi–ma–mi   I. 1. Amadis, Florestan
  D mi–ma   I. 2. Corisande, Florestan
    A mi   I. 3. Orianne, Florestan, Corisande
      C   I. 4. Combattants

        F   Prelude
        F   II. 1. Arcabonne
        F   II. 2. Arcabonne, Arcalaus
  D mi

G mi   II. 3. Arcalaus
        B♭   II. 4. Amadis
G mi–ma   II. 5–6. Corisande, Amadis, etc.
G mi–mi–ma   II. 7. Demons, monsters, nymphs etc.
G mi   II. 7. Amadis, 'nymphs', 'shepherds'

      C mi–ma   III. 1. Captives, gaolers

    (A mi)

        F   III. 2. Captives, gaolers, Arcabonne
      C mi   III. 3. Captives, gaolers, Arcabonne,
                           shade of Ardan
      C ma   Prelude
      C ma   III. 4. Arcabonne, Amadis, and others;
                           recitative followed by ritournelle
    A mi   Chorus and Ballet

      F mi   IV. 1. Arcalaus, Arcabonne
G   IV. 2. Oriane
  D ma   IV. 3. Oriane, Arcalaus
  D mi   IV. 4. Oriane, Amadis
  D ma   IV. 5. Oriane, Amadis, Arcalaus,
                           Arcabonne
    A ma   IV. 6. Urgande, Arcalaus, Arcabonne,
D ma   Amadis, Oriane and others

      F ma   V. 1. Urgande, Amadis
      F mi   V. 2. Oriane, Amadis
    C mi–ma
G   V. 3. Oriane, Amadis, Urgande
G   V. 4. Oriane, Amadis, Urgande,
                           Florestan, Corisande
    C ma–mi–ma–mi–ma   V. 5. Chorus and dances

hensible overall structure, either closed or interlocked, whereas this opera presents an additive process, from C to F to D to B flat to G minor. This, added to the fact that the autograph manuscript, as Professor E. J. Dent pointed out in the preface to his 1925 edition of the opera, 'disappeared at a very early date . . . and . . . considerable confusion has taken place',

Purcell—*Dido and Aeneas*

C mi		Overture
C mi–ma		'Shake the cloud . . . Fear no danger'
	E mi	Cupid only
C		'Pursue thy conquest'
		'To the hills and the vales'
I. i	F mi	Weird sisters . . . 'harm's our delight'
C		'Ho, ho, ho'
ii	F	'Ho, ho, ho'
	D mi	'But ere we this perform'
F		'In our deep vaulted cell'
II.	D mi–ma	'Thanks to these lonesome vales'
		'Haste, haste'
	(A mi)	'Stay, Prince'
III.	B♭	'Come away . . . Destruction's our delight'
	G mi	'Your counsel all is urged in vain'
	(B♭)	'Great minds against themselves conspire'
	G mi	'When I am laid in earth'
	G mi	'With drooping wings'

may give us leave to wonder whether in nearly three hundred years of editorial tinkering something of structural importance has been mislaid.

The large-scale religious works of the period follow the same structural patterns as those of opera. The overall structure of *Messiah* has already been mentioned, and we may add to that mention the following observations. There are three appearances of the E–A double-tonality unit (major or minor, variously, in both cases): from the overture to 'And the glory of

Handel—*Messiah*

		Overture
	E mi	

I. E ma / A

D mi / G mi / D / B mi / G / D / C / B♭ / F / B♭

- 'Comfort ye'/'Every valley'
- 'And the glory'
- 'Thus saith the Lord'
- 'And He shall purify'
- 'O thou that tellest'
- 'The people that sat in darkness'
- 'For unto us a Child is born'
- 'Pastoral Symphony'
- 'Glory to God'
- 'Rejoice!'
- 'Come unto Him'
- 'His yoke is easy'

II. G mi / E♭ / F mi–ma / C mi / E mi / A / F / D ma–mi / B♭ / G mi / E♭ / C / A mi / D

- 'Behold the Lamb of God'
- 'He was despised'
- 'And with His stripes'/'All we, like sheep'
- 'He trusted in God'
- 'Let us break their bonds'
- 'Thou didst not leave'
- 'Lift up your heads!'
- 'Let all the angels of God'
- 'Thou art gone up on high'
- 'The Lord gave the Word'
- 'How beautiful are the feet'
- 'Their word is gone out'
- 'Why do the people?'
- 'He shall break them'
- 'Hallelujah!'

III. E ma / A mi / D / E♭ / G mi / D

- 'I know that my Redeemer liveth'
- 'For since by man came death'
- 'The trumpet shall sound'
- 'O Death!...O grave!'
- 'If God be for us'
- 'Worthy is the Lamb'
- Amen

the Lord', from 'Let us break their bonds asunder' to 'But Thou didst not leave His soul in hell' in Part II, and from 'I know that my Redeemer liveth' to 'For since by man came death' at the beginning of Part III. The weight of the elements composing the D structure—'Thus saith the Lord'—'But who may abide the day of His coming?'—'Glory to God!'—'Let all the angels of God'—'Thou art gone up on high'—'Hallelujah!' —'The trumpet shall sound'—'Worthy is the Lamb'—'Amen'— is so enormous that we may feel justified in regarding the work as essentially D, with the interlocking introduction E/A that I have suggested. But equally—and it does not matter which

Bach—*Hohe Messe*

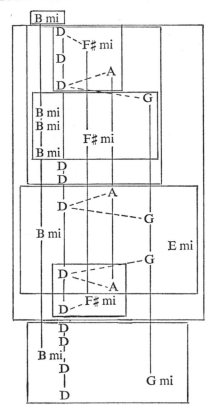

'Kyrie eleison'
'Christe eleison'
'Kyrie eleison'
'Gloria in excelsis'
'Laudamus te'
'Gratias agimus'
'Domine Deus'

'Qui tollis'

'Qui sedes'
'Quoniam tu solus'
'Cum Sancto Spiritu'
'Credo in unum Deum'
'Patrem omnipotentem'
'Et in unum Dominum'
'Et incarnatus'
'Crucifixus'

'Et resurrexit'
'Et in spiritum Sanctum'
'Confiteor'
'Et exspecto'
'Sanctus'
'Osanna'
'Benedictus qui venit'
'Osanna'
'Agnus Dei'
'Dona nobis pacem'

solution one chooses, as long as the comprehensibility of the structure is granted—it may be considered an interlocking E–A/D structure overall.

Whichever of these two formulations of the overall structure we choose, the D structure encloses a G minor structure enclosing an interlocking C/E flat structure, of which the C element encloses a B flat structure enclosing an F structure.

Bach's *Hohe Messe* creates an interlocking B minor/D major structure in which the key of D is much more in evidence than B minor. The overall structure would be better expressed as a D structure in which the home key has frequently associated with it its relative minor.

The tonal structure of Bach's *St Matthew Passion* is shown on pages 42–3.

We can reduce the complete tonal diagram to the following outline:

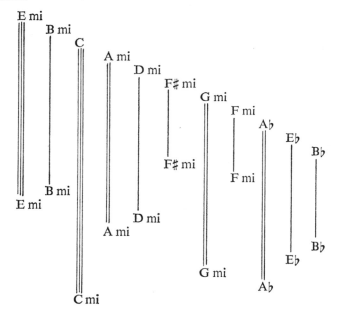

from which it is easier to recognise the tonal shape of the work. The basic structure interlocks E minor/C minor, in which the

Bach—*St Matthew Passion*

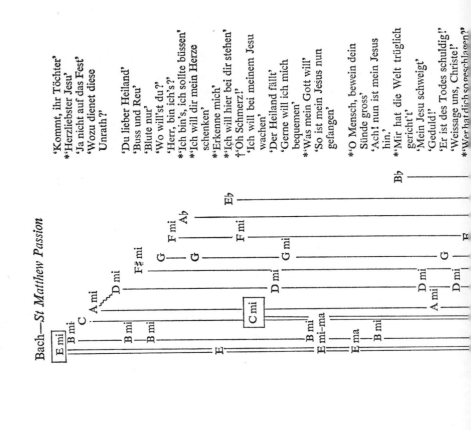

'Komm, ihr Töchter'
*'Herzliebster Jesu'
'Ja nicht auf das Fest'
'Wozu dienet diese Unrath?'

'Du lieber Heiland'
'Buss und Reu'
'Blute nur'
'Wo will'st du?'
'Herr, bin ich's?'
*'Ich bin's, ich sollte büssen'
*'Ich will dir mein Herze schenken'
*'Erkenne mich'
*'Ich will hier bei dir stehen'
†'Oh Schmerz!'
'Ich will bei meinem Jesu wachen'
'Der Heiland fällt'
'Gerne will ich mich bequemen'
*'Was mein Gott will'
'So ist mein Jesus nun gefangen'

*'O Mensch, bewein dein Sünde gross'
'Ach! nun ist mein Jesus hin.'
*'Mir hat die Welt trüglich gericht't'
'Mein Jesu schweigt'
'Geduld!'
'Er ist des Todes schuldig!'
'Weissage uns, Christe!'
*'Wer hat dich so geschlagen?'

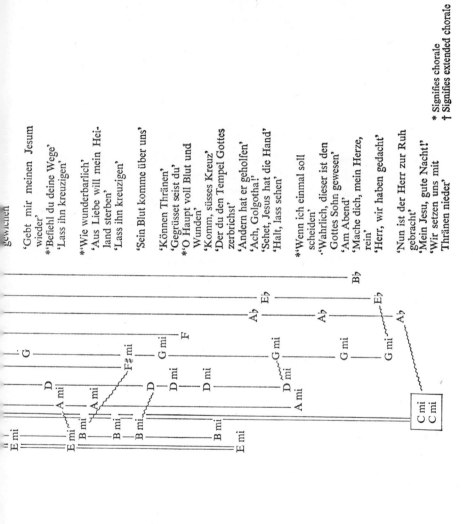

'Gebt mir meinen Jesum wieder'
*'Befiehl du deine Wege'
'Lass ihn kreuzigen'

*'Wie wunderbarlich'
'Aus Liebe will mein Heiland sterben'
'Lass ihn kreuzigen'

'Sein Blut komme über uns'

'Können Thränen'
'Grüsset seist du'
*'O Haupt voll Blut und Wunden'
'Komm, süsses Kreuz'
'Der du den Tempel Gottes zerbrichst'
'Andern hat er geholfen'
'Ach, Golgotha!'
'Sehet, Jesus hat die Hand'
'Halt, lass sehen'

*'Wenn ich einmal soll scheiden'
'Wahrlich, dieser ist den Gottes Sohn gewesen'
'Am Abend'
'Mache dich, mein Herze, rein'
'Herr, wir haben gedacht'

'Nun ist der Herr zur Ruh gebracht'
'Mein Jesu, gute Nacht!'
'Wir setzen uns mit Thränen nieder'

* Signifies chorale
† Signifies extended chorale

E minor element encloses a B minor structure. The C–C minor structure produced by the appearance of C major ('Ja, nicht auf das Fest') some time before the C minor structure begins, encloses an interlocking A minor/A major structure, of which the A minor element encloses a D minor structure, which encloses an F minor structure. The A flat structure has associated with it, forming a double-tonality unit, the key of G major–minor, which in turn has interlocking with it an F minor–major structure. The G major–minor/A flat structure encloses an E flat structure which encloses a B flat structure.

The *St Matthew Passion* is a particularly striking example of the interaction of tonal structure and narrative which is possible in such structures. For the key of C minor that begins the second tonal structure of the main interlocking process is an expression of the text: 'Ich will bei meinem Jesum wachen'. The connection of this with the text of the final chorus, 'Wir setzen uns mit Tränen nieder', needs no emphasising.

The *St John Passion* is an interlocking G minor/E flat structure. The first appearance of E flat (the bass arioso 'Betrachte, meine Seel' ') is supported by the following C minor aria for tenor ('Erwäge'), and this procedure re-appears in a reversing-end process (a mirror, but applied only to the two outer members of the structure) at the end of the work (the chorus 'Ruht wohl' (C minor) and the final chorale (E flat)). It is not of basic structural importance, but is of interest, that the one other appearance of E flat—the chorale 'In meines Herzens Grunde'—is followed after a brief recitative by the C *major* chorus 'Lasset uns den nicht zerteilen'. Thus in this work E flat/C constitutes an invariable double-tonality unit which is itself the second main structural tonality.

CLASSICAL DRAMATIC STRUCTURE

Professor E. J. Dent pointed out in *Mozart's Operas* that 'Haydn was always convinced that his operas were his greatest

Bach—*St John Passion*

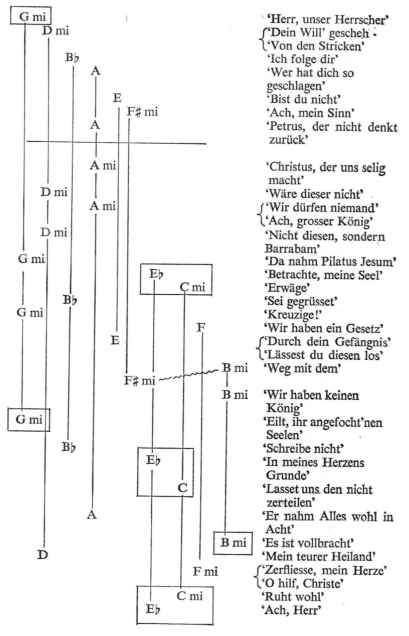

works', but that 'attempts to resurrect them have only proved their insignificance'. The validity of this estimate may be contested, but, for whatever reason, it is true that they have not held the stage. Thus classical opera, taken as works still performed, is limited to the last operas of Mozart and Beethoven's *Fidelio*.

The obvious tonal fact about Mozart's still-performed operas is that all of them—and this 'all' is unique among major opera composers—are 'closed' structures ending in the key in which they began. This simplifies the problem for the analyst, since at the worst he can only get the internal structure all wrong. But it is also apt to mislead him into supposing that, having announced the obvious, he may recline at his ease and ignore what happens between—for example—the two D majors which bound *Le Nozze di Figaro*.

A glance at the diagram opposite of all the keys that constitute that opera (excluding the tonally irrelevant recitative) will show that Mozart used the same series of keys in the same sorts of relationship throughout it. Even granting that structural tonal functions may be either consciously or unconsciously devised by the composer, it is difficult to imagine that Mozart—perhaps the most perfectly equipped composer as to both talent and training in our tradition—was unaware of those keys and their relationship. But it is not of basic importance whether we regard Mozart's part as having been conscious or unconscious: what is basically important is that the *listener* can become conscious of this tonal structure (though he is very unlikely to in the course of aesthetic apprehension).

Looking again at the diagram, we can add to the bald but true statement that *Figaro* is a D structure by noting that the D structure encloses a G structure and that almost every time G appears it has B flat with it; that the G structure encloses a B flat structure which encloses an E flat structure (or if you like a double-tonality-unit F/E flat structure); and that the E flat structure encloses a C structure. Further we may observe that the first element of the E flat structure consists of three state-

Mozart—*Le Nozze di Figaro*

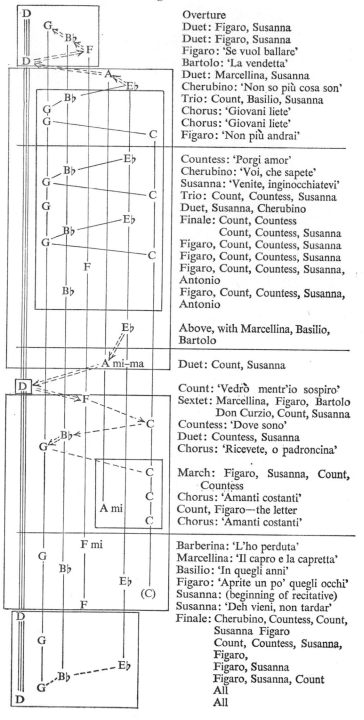

Overture
Duet: Figaro, Susanna
Duet: Figaro, Susanna
Figaro: 'Se vuol ballare'
Bartolo: 'La vendetta'
Duet: Marcellina, Susanna
Cherubino: 'Non so più cosa son'
Trio: Count, Basilio, Susanna
Chorus: 'Giovani liete'
Chorus: 'Giovani liete'
Figaro: 'Non più andrai'

Countess: 'Porgi amor'
Cherubino: 'Voi, che sapete'
Susanna: 'Venite, inginocchiatevi'
Trio: Count, Countess, Susanna
Duet, Susanna, Cherubino
Finale: Count, Countess
      Count, Countess, Susanna
Figaro, Count, Countess, Susanna
Figaro, Count, Countess, Susanna
Figaro, Count, Countess, Susanna, Antonio
Figaro, Count, Countess, Susanna, Antonio

Above, with Marcellina, Basilio, Bartolo

Duet: Count, Susanna

Count: 'Vedrò mentr'io sospiro'
Sextet: Marcellina, Figaro, Bartolo
      Don Curzio, Count, Susanna
Countess: 'Dove sono'
Duet: Countess, Susanna
Chorus: 'Ricevete, o padroncina'

March: Figaro, Susanna, Count, Countess
Chorus: 'Amanti costanti'
Count, Figaro—the letter
Chorus: 'Amanti costanti'

Barberina: 'L'ho perduta'
Marcellina: 'Il capro e la capretta'
Basilio: 'In quegli anni'
Figaro: 'Aprite un po' quegli occhi'
Susanna: (beginning of recitative)
Susanna: 'Deh vieni, non tardar'
Finale: Cherubino, Countess, Count, Susanna Figaro
      Count, Countess, Susanna, Figaro,
      Figaro, Susanna
      Figaro, Susanna, Count
All
All

ments of the group E flat followed by B flat-with-G followed by C, the series of statements ending with a final appearance of E flat; that the G-with-B flat which occurs soon after the beginning of Act IV is also associated with E flat and a brief reference to C; and that the last appearance of E flat in the opera is also associated with G and B flat.

Three appearances of the key of A (one major, one minor, and the middle one minor-to-major) bring us to the matter of what we have called 'running structure'. This is the structure which makes its appeal to the ear in the normal unfolding of the time-sequence in which the opera is heard (using 'heard' to mean, not heard necessarily—or even probably—in the act of aesthetic apprehension, but heard in the cold act of listening for structural analysis).

No-one, presumably, would deny that we shall hear the first group of five tonalities as a D structure, and the eye will be immediately caught, as it surveys the diagram, by the single appearance of D as the second tonality of Act III (the Count's aria, 'Vedrò mentr'io sospiro'). If the materials between these two appearances of D proved to have a clear-cut structure of their own it would be convenient; and the uncommon convenience of the pattern created by these structures is straight away apparent.

For immediately after Bartolo's 'La vendetta'—the last element of the first D structure—Marcellina and Susanna sing their duet in A, and just before the Count sings his 'Vedrò mentr'io sospiro' in D he and Susanna sing their duet in A. Almost anything of reasonably compendious length, and things of a good deal greater length if they are themselves clearly structured, reach the ear as closed tonal structures if they begin and end in the same key. Thus the whole area between the two appearances of D is an A structure.

Furthermore, immediately after the duet between Susanna and Marcellina in A, Cherubino sings his 'Non so più cosa son' in E flat, and just before the Count and Susanna sing their duet in A the septet of major principals sings its 'Voi Signor! che giusto siete' (and so on to the end of the act) in E flat.

Thus the previously noted A structure is what we have called a 'reversing-end' procedure, starting with A–E flat and finishing with E flat–A.

But this is still not all. For the reversing-end process extends itself so that we have the mirror-process, from the start of Act I to the middle of Act III:

G B♭ F D A E♭   B flat   E♭ A D F (C) B♭ G

As if to emphasise the reality of this mirror, the rest of Act III consists of a self-contained C structure with A minor as its middle section. The C major which interrupts the consequent of the mirror (The Countess's 'Dove sono') forms the first element of a C structure made up of 'Dove sono' and the march and chorus, interlocking with that consequent. It is the nature of the first appearance of the second element in an interlocking structure to 'interrupt' the first element, and this example is no more upsetting than any other.

Setting aside now this mirror aspect of the structure, which is ornamental, we have as the main structure so far the process D A D: the beginning perhaps of a tonal rondo. For if we could find a tonality, or a series of tonalities, following the third-Act D, to fulfil the requirement of 'opposite tonal relation' we should have, together with the final D structure, the completion of that rondo.

The principle of 'opposite tonal relation', which is presented on page 79 in relation to the instrumental structures characteristic of the period under discussion, can be stated briefly as demanding that, if the second main tonal area of such a structure is on the bright side of the first, the third main tonal area must be on the dark side of the second. Thus what I have called a 'tonal rondo' would consist (and *does* consist in practice from Couperin to Brahms) of the tonal relationships: home—bright—home—dark-side-of-the-bright—home. We need only to glance at the *Figaro* diagram to see that what follows the third-Act D is a clearly structured tonality of F, extending straight to the final appearance of D.

Mozart's other late operas are all of this basic structural type: a closed tonal structure having definable structures comprehensibly related within it. Those of his earlier operas which are otherwise constructed are discussed on pages 198–200.

STRUCTURES OF ARIAS AND ENSEMBLES

The structures of individual arias and ensembles in his operas are of interest to a consideration of tonal structure generally. For not only do they represent a greater number of structural types than do the instrumental works of the period, but also they make use of recurrent patterns tonally with little regard for any sort of thematic symmetry.

That this should occur in opera is understandable, because the articulation which in an instrumental work is supplied by a recurrent theme can be supplied in opera by narrative considerations. This is indeed the area of the musical structure in which narrative considerations can pre-eminently play a part.

In *Le Nozze di Figaro* the following generalised structures appear in individual set pieces:

1. $A_{1-\text{dom ch}}/B_{2-1}C_1$
2. $A_1B_2/\text{dom susp } A_1 \ B_1$
3. $A_{1-2 \text{ or dom ch}}$ (with or without B) $\left/ \begin{array}{ll} \text{dom susp} & \text{most or} \\ \text{or SOTR} & \text{part of} \\ \text{or 1} & A_1 \end{array}\right.$
4. $A_{1-\text{dom ch}}B_2/\text{SOTR}_4A^1_1$
5. $1 - 2/4 - 1$ monothematic
6. $1 - 2/1 - 4 - 1$ (i.e., tonally a rondo but without the thematic character of rondo)
7. $A_1B_2A_1/\text{SOTR}_4 \ C_1$ (feeling like a rondo, but lacking the final thematic return; cf. the same structure in the last movement of the C major String Quintet)
8. $A_1 \ B_2 \ C_1/D_4$ reference to $A_1 \ E_1$ (tonally a rondo but with almost complete thematic diversity; cf., for this characteristic, but not as rondos, the first movements of the first two piano concertos of Beethoven)
9. $A_1B_2/C_{1-2-4-1}$

10. $A_1 B_2$ link to return of $_1 CD_1$ containing refs to A and B
    as well as the concerto-like structures:

11. A (as OST)$_1$

    $A^1{}_{1-\text{dom ch}}B^1{}_1A^2{}_1$ coda on part of A_1

12. A (as OST)$_1$

    $A^1{}_{1-2}$ ext$_{-\text{dom ch}}$ B_1 ref to A_1 coda on new material

There is, in addition, in Figaro's 'Se vuol ballare, Signor
contino', an example of an interlocking minuet-and-trio:

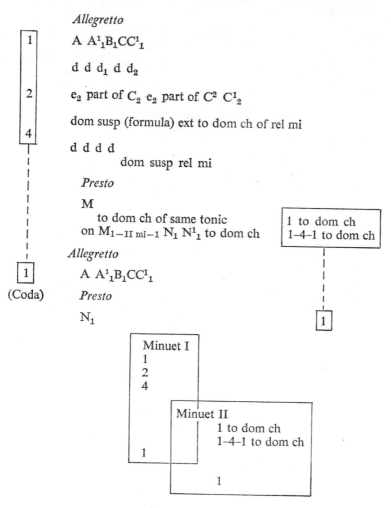

BEETHOVEN

If the hypothesis that dramatic musical structure is essentially and audibly tonal were to prove untenable, one would surely expect it to do so in the one opera of Beethoven. As an instrumental writer venturing into a foreign field, he might not be expected to have in his bones those traditions which constitute a common procedure among composers who were first of all operatic writers.

Beethoven —*Fidelio*

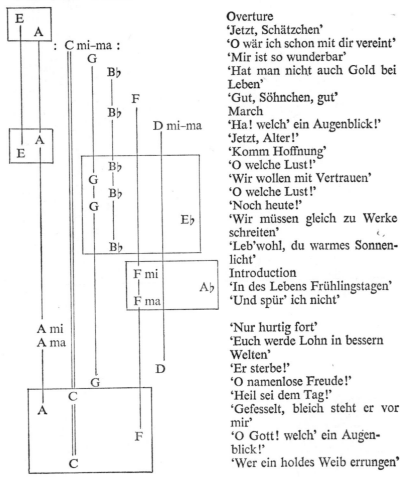

Overture
'Jetzt, Schätzchen'
'O wär ich schon mit dir vereint'
'Mir ist so wunderbar'
'Hat man nicht auch Gold bei Leben'
'Gut, Söhnchen, gut'
March
'Ha! welch' ein Augenblick!'
'Jetzt, Alter!'
'Komm Hoffnung'
'O welche Lust!'
'Wir wollen mit Vertrauen'
'O welche Lust!'
'Noch heute!'
'Wir müssen gleich zu Werke schreiten'
'Leb'wohl, du warmes Sonnenlicht'
Introduction
'In des Lebens Frühlingstagen'
'Und spür' ich nicht'

'Nur hurtig fort'
'Euch werde Lohn in bessern Welten'
'Er sterbe!'
'O namenlose Freude!'
'Heil sei dem Tag!'
'Gefesselt, bleich steht er vor mir'
'O Gott! welch' ein Augenblick!'
'Wer ein holdes Weib errungen'

Yet the overall structure of *Fidelio* (p. 52) is perfectly clear as an interlocking structure of which the first element is a reversing-end E/A structure, in the manner of Handel's *Sosarme*, and the second a large C structure which stretches from the repeated C minor–major structure of 'O wär' ich schon mit dir vereint', near the beginning of the opera, to the C—A—F—C (home—bright—dark—home) structure of the second Act finale. This large-scale C structure contains a G structure which encloses an interlocking B flat/D structure, the D of which encloses an A—E—B flat/F—A (home—bright—dark—home) structure of which the A—E is the 'reversing' end of the interlocking process which starts with the overture.

The structure of *Fidelio* before Beethoven changed the key of the overture from C to E was a closed C structure in which the key of A at the beginning of Act I, though it had not its present character as the start of a 'reversing-end' process, remained the start of the large-scale A structure which—then as now—extended from immediately after the overture to almost immediately before the final C major chorus. There would in fact, in view of the very large scale of the C structure which constitutes most of the opera, be no objection to calling it a closed C structure still, with the interlocking reversing-end A/E process regarded as a start ornamentally remote from the main key of the work (cf. *Messiah*, p. 39).

WAGNER'S MUSIC-DRAMA

Wagner's tonal design can be analysed into three functions and an added attraction. These are: (i) the main tonal structure; (ii) smaller, interlocking tonal structures; (iii) subsidiary tonal threads (sometimes very important, even though subordinate to the whole); and (iv) (the added attraction), keys of specific meaning subjective to the composer.

Analysis of *Die Meistersinger* will show all these in action, this particular example being chosen as a mature work which is tonally more clear-cut than *Tristan* or *Parsifal*. But its being more clear-cut does not mean that it is built on different structural principles from the harmonically more complex works. They conform precisely to the same simplicity of outline (though naturally not to the same outline).

There follows a tabulation of the tonalities in *Die Meistersinger* in relation to its characters and events.

Tonality	Characters or events	Scene
C E E♭ C	Prelude and Chorale	1
B♭	Walther, Eva, Magdalena	
C	Walther, Eva, Magdalena, David	
D B♭ E♭ mod D	Walther, David	2
G	Apprentices	
F A F	Pogner and Beckmesser with Walther	3
E minor	Roll-call of Mastersingers 'In deutschen Landen'	
F	Pogner's Prize	
E	Discussion of Pogner's offer	3
G	Sachs' comment	3
E	End of discussion	3
B♭	Introduction of Walther by Pogner	3
D	'Am stillen Herd'	3
B♭	Beckmesser as Marker	3
C	Kothner reads the *Leges*	3
F	'So rief der Lenz'	3
chrom on E♭ E♭ F	Discussion by Mastersingers	3
F	Verse 2 in confusion	3
Act II		
G	Prelude and Apprentices	1
B♭	Pogner and Eva	2
G	Eva, Magdalena and Sachs	2
G	Sachs	3
F E F	Sachs	3
A♭ F A♭ (E♭)	Sachs and Eva	4
(A)	Sachs and Eva concerning Walther	4
B♭	Sachs and Eva concerning Walther	4
G	Sachs satisfied	4
	Eva and Magdalena concerning Beckmesser	4
A	Walther and Eva	5
B F B F mod B	Love-music and Watchman	5
B♭G B♭G B♭G B♭E G B♭B G	Cobbler's Song and Beckmesser	5

Tonality	Characters or events	Scene
G	Beckmesser and Riot	6 and 7
B F E	Watchman	7
Act III		
G	Prelude	1
mod	David with Sachs	1
DCD A mi D mi F D mi	David with Sachs	1
(B mod: A♭E C)	Sachs	1
E♭ B♭ E♭ G mod E♭	Sachs and Walther	2
C	Prize-song verses 1 and 2	2
E♭	Conclusion of scent	2
D ma mod to mi	Beckmesser	3
D mi E♭D E♭D	Beckmesser and Sachs	3
(A♭ mod to C)	Sachs	3
A♭ B A♭	Sachs and Eva (Walther in B)	4
C	Prize-song verse 3	4
B♭	Sachs covering the confusion	4
G	(Cobbler) Eva, followed by Sachs	4
mod B♭D	'jetzt schnell zur Taufe' and 'Ein Kind'	4
C	Sachs 'Eine Meisterweise' (tune of Kothner's 'Leges' in Act I)	4
G♭	Quintet	4
mod: B (Walther) E A (at some length) C	Transformation from shop to meadow	5
F C A mi C F	Guilds	5
B♭	Apprentices	5
C	Entry of the Mastersingers	5
G	'Wach auf!' to 'Heil Nürnbergs Sachs'	5
C	'Heil!'	
A mi to D	'Wahn' music to 'Euch macht ihr's leicht'	5
G	Sachs	5
C	Sachs	5
E♭	Beckmesser comes forward	5
C	'Silentium!'	
E mi C E mi (ma at end)	Beckmesser's song	5
D ma to C	Walther comes forward	5
C	Prize-song verse 3	5
	Subsequent expressions of satisfaction	
F	Pogner gives the chain	5
G♭	Walther refuses it (gazing at Eva)	5

Tonality	Characters or events	Scene
C G F C chrom coda	Sachs 'Verachtet mir die Meister nicht'	5
C	'Ehrt eure deutschen Meister'	5

Although we shall find that Wagner's procedures are essentially the same as those of his predecessors (those of Mozart in the case of *Die Meistersinger*, which is a 'closed' C major structure) their analysis is complicated by the continuous character of the music, and the presence therefore of large areas of tonally indeterminate material corresponding structurally to the recitative of Baroque and Classical opera. There is in addition the problem of keys which at first sight create no tonal structure simple enough in outline to be readily recognisable.

The type of problem that besets us is shown at once in Act I. The prelude is straightforward; its tonal structure being C major, E major, brief return to C (enough to establish the relative darkness of the following E flat) E flat major, C major, i.e., home—bright—briefly home—dark—home. It runs into the first scene of Act I in the manner that Wagner used consistently from *Das Rheingold* onwards, presenting no problem of tonal analysis because the tonality of the prelude continues until the end of the chorale.

But then what?

Walther's 'Verweilt! Ein Wort—ein einzig Wort!' begins a section in B flat, and, since B flat recurs when Walther is introduced to the Mastersingers by Pogner and also (relatively briefly but extremely decisively) when Beckmesser goes to the Marker's box, and is followed by Kothner's C major reading of the rules, we are faced with the possibility that the body of this act is a B flat structure within a C major one, with the F major of 'So rief der Lenz' the next main tonal factor of the work.

This interpretation remains one not to be lightly discarded, yet we must consider two factors which militate against it: first, that, despite this tidy B flat diagram, one's memory is tugged at not by B flat but by D major in the first part of this act, and second that Scene 3 begins an important F major section in which the nominal-roll of the Mastersingers is called and Pogner announces the prize he intends to bestow. Were we to assume the B flat hypothesis, this F major would become an element in a G major—F major—E major—G (home—dark—bright—home) structure extending from the apprentices' 'Aller End' ist doch David der allergescheit'st' to Sachs' '. . . wer nichts weiss von der Tabulatur' and its coda, finishing and dissipating on 'mein' ich, Hans Sachs!' This G major structure does in fact exist, and is an example of the interlocking structures which have been mentioned and will later require examination; but, since Scene 3 continues to the end of the act and begins and ends in F major, the proposal that its first F major is primarily a subordinate part of another structure seems unlikely.

What if we assume this F major scene as the decisive tonal factor in the act? The tonal structure of the scene then becomes:

F	Pogner–roll-call–Pogner
E G E	Discussion
B♭ D B♭	Walther introduced–'Am stillen Herd'–Beckmesser Marker
C	Kothner reads the rules
F chrom E♭ F	'So rief der Lenz'

This is a satisfactory structure in itself, and equally so whether one regards it as 'home—bright—dark—bright—home' or as 'home—bright—dark—home', with C major interlocking from the beginning of the act. If we accept it as decisive we must return to problems at the beginning of the act.

We left the importance of B flat undecided, and it is now clear that this key is not part of the main tonal structure in the sense of our category 1; for the only way to make it so would be to undermine the importance of F major, which we have already decided to accept as the second main tonality of the act. We may therefore now take full cognizance of the fact, previously noticed but pushed aside by other considerations, that the first appearance of B flat (Walther's approach to Eva in the church) is followed by further lengthy and thematically clear-cut music in C major, which we may readily accept as the finish of the tonal structure that began with the prelude.

There remains in this act the tonality of D major, which we specified as important because of its strong memory impression. Had the B flat hypothesis proved tenable, a large D major structure stretching from David's instruction of Walther to 'Am stillen Herd' would have constituted a unit lying comfortably inside the B flat structure. Now that 'Am stillen Herd' lies within the established F major structure, its connection with the previous D major music (a connection which, the two sections being so distinctive, cannot be ignored) is an interlocking structure, and the first D major (David-Walther) must be re-classified as a factor less important than we previously thought it. Yet it is still important as not only the first element of this interlocking structure but also the first element in a 'subsidiary tonal thread' (category 3). The apprentices' G major which follows is partly a process of tonal transition to F major, partly the first element of a structure interlocking with the beginning of the F major structure, and partly an element in a subsidiary tonal thread in a key which is also one of the main structural tonalities of the opera.

The structural framework of the Act is then:

C   Prelude; to the departure of Eva and Madalena.
F   Pogner and the Mastersingers to the end of the Act.

Still to be considered are the relation to one another of the act's interlocking structures, and the 'subsidiary tonal threads'.

Interlocking structures
(a) A C major structure (which may also be considered as on the lower level of a 'subsidiary tonal thread') stretching from the beginning of the prelude to Kothner's reading of the rules, interlocking with the F major structure of Scene 3. (b) The B flat structure already referred to, beginning with Walther's approach to Eva and ending with a tonal *ABA* structure having Walther's introduction to the Mastersingers as its start and

Beckmesser as Marker for its finish. This B flat structure interlocks at one end with the main C major structure at the start of
the work, and at the other with the F major of Scene 3, the
final smaller *ABA* B flat structure forming a middle section to
the F major structure. (c) The D major structure also previously
referred to, starting with David's instructions to Walther and
ending with 'Am stillen Herd'. It interlocks with the large F
structure and forms a middle section to the large B flat structure.

These three are the important interlocking structures of Act I,
but there are two more which, though small-scale, are plain to
be heard: (d) a G—F—E—G structure, referred to above, beginning with the apprentices and ending with Sachs' comment on
Pogner's offer interlocking with the F structure; and (e) an
E—G—E structure beginning with the Mastersingers' 'discussion of Pogner's offer', having Sachs' comment in the middle,
and finishing with the end of the discussion, interlocking with
the G—F—E—G structure. Both these, besides being interlocking structures, are parts of subsidiary tonal threads. For
the key of E, though much less important than G, continues to
make unobtrusive appearances throughout the work, finally
establishing its importance as the key of Beckmesser's song in
Act III and showing why it should have been used for the
Abgesang of the prize-song on its first appearance in the prelude.

Subsidiary tonal threads
The keys of D major, G major and E (major or minor) have
already been referred to in this capacity, and there are two more.
B flat major has been important in Act I and remains so in
Act II; and E flat, which first appeared for the apprentices'
dance in the prelude, reappears briefly as the beginning of a
process of modulation in the middle section of David's conversation with Walther, and is used for the middle section (at first
chromatically *on* E flat and then, as Sachs breaks in, specifically)
in the Mastersingers' discussion of the first verse of 'So rief der
Lenz'. It then makes a modest appearance in Act II, after the
sizeable A flat conversation between Sachs and Eva, but

conserves its strength for the scene in Act III between Sachs and Walther in which the prize-song comes into being.

Our finds for Act I can now be tabulated thus:

Wagner—*Meistersinger Act I*

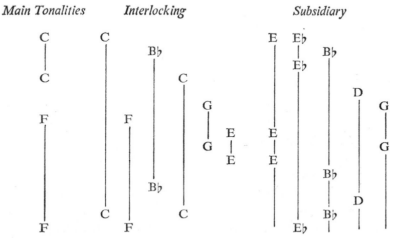

| *Main Tonalities* | *Interlocking* | | *Subsidiary* |

Act II is somewhat simpler to analyse because it is a tonally closed movement in G major, the first element of which is formed by the prelude and the music of the apprentices, and the closing element by the riot after Beckmesser's serenade. Within this lies a structure with rondo-like tonal characteristics, the corner-stones and key-stone being the consecutive keys of B flat and G: first when Pogner and Eva appear and converse, next when Sachs makes contemptuous comments about Walther in order to satisfy himself as to Eva's feelings, and finally the large section beginning with the cobbler's song and ending with Beckmesser's serenade. We shall often come across this tendency of Wagner's to use two keys in succession as a tonal unit: we have already seen it in the fourth interlocking structure, where the keys Bb C are used as the outer elements of a structure in which the D major unit forms the middle section; in this same Act B major and its tonal opposite F major are so used; and in Act III D major and C major. The Bb G grouping now under discussion reappears as the point in Act III which completes the tonal movement of the whole work, and leads to the structural return of C major which arches back to the establishment of that tonality at the beginning of the work. Thus it creates an internal unit consisting of the whole of Act II and of Act III up to this point. We shall return to this in discussing the overall tonal structure of the work.

The structure of this Act is thus defined by the three appearances of B♭G, the centre one flanked by the A♭ of the conversation between Sachs and Eva and the A major of that between Eva and Walther.

It remains to mention two interlocking structures: G B♭ G as just mentioned, at the beginning, interlocking with the main B flat G structure; and a structure based on the combined tonalities B and F, extending from the love-music of Walther and Eva followed by the Watchman's music, to the reappearance of the Watchman to disperse the riot—this structure interlocking with the end of the large B flat G structure. And two subsidiary threads: F major, harking back to the tonality of second importance in the first act, and E major, which appears in Sachs' soliloquy, again towards the end of the discussion between Sachs and Beckmesser just before the latter sings his serenade, and finally as the main constituent of the coda to the Act.

Our findings in Act II are then:

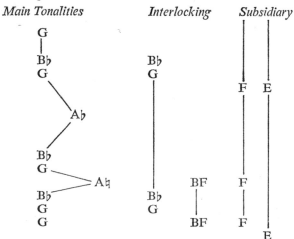

Act III, as we have already discovered, is tonally a continuation of Act II until it reaches the B flat of Sachs' monologue covering the confusion of Walther and Eva after the third verse of the prize-song, and the G major of Eva's and Sachs' ensuing endearments. Thereafter it foreshadows the structural return of the home key in Sachs' 'Eine Meisterweise' (to the tune of Kothner's reading of the rules in Act I), then modulates away in a lengthy introduction to the actual structural return which begins with the entry of the Mastersingers.

After the G major of the prelude and the modulatory material of David's monologue, his 'Am Jordan Sanct Johannes stand' begins a huge D major structural element which finishes at Beckmesser's ecstatic departure with Walther's poem, and has the large E flat structure of Sachs' conversation with Walther as its middle section. This dominant-key second tonal area in a G major structure is balanced (in a classical home-key— bright side—dark side—home-key structure) by an ABA tonal structure consisting of A flat (Sachs' conversation with Eva), B major (Walther's appearance at the door) and, briefly but decisively, A flat: the whole structure enclosed in C major consisting, before the A flat structure, of the end of Sachs' comment on Beckmesser and, after it, of the third verse of the prize-song. This C major structure, with A♭ in the middle, completes an interlocking C major structure which began in the course of the E flat material, and the first structural element of the act is completed, as has already been pointed out, by the reappearance of B flat followed by G, in the music of Sachs and Eva.

After a brief modulation through B flat to D—keys whose structural functions in this work are now familiar to us—the last structural element of the work begins: an element on so vast a scale that it can well perform the function of balancing the large C major structure with which the opera opens.

It begins by moving from the C major of Sachs' 'Eine Meisterweise', through the G flat major of the quintet (one of only two G flats in all); through the transformation from shop to meadow by means of modulation on the bright side of C

(G flat having had theoretically the complete ambiguity of the tonal opposite; but actually, because of its downward chromatic approach, sounding dark) the music of the various guilds beginning and ending in F major; and the apprentices' dance in B flat—both on the dark side of the preceding materials; to C major again for the entry of the Mastersingers. A bright-side section in G major is formed by the music beginning with 'Wach auf!' and ending with Sachs' 'das Nürnberg . . . die Kunst und ihre Meister ehrt!' C major returns as Pogner thanks him, and forms a structure ending with 'Silentium!', E flat constituting a middle section as Beckmesser mounts the mound. A tonal balance in this larger C major unit is provided by the dark-side E minor of Beckmesser's rendering of Walther's poem, the Mastersingers' comments making an internal return to C, and Sachs bringing it back first to E minor and thence, through still another brief return to C, to E major. We are now on the bright side of the second tonality (E minor) of the C major structure, and thereby conforming to classical usage in the frequent return of a bright-side key or keys immediately before the structural return of the home key. Walther advances in D major, the Mastersingers make their admiring comments on Sachs' slyness in C major, and Walther, after a brief chromatic excursion on the 'selige Morgentraum–Deutweise' music, sings his song as the first element of the C major structure which finishes at the same time the larger C major structure on which we have been engaged, and the work. We need not pay much attention to the internal structure of the first part of this unit, since the F major in which Pogner gives the chain and the G flat major in which Walther attempts to refuse it are both ornamental to the structure; but the place of F major in the opera is now sufficiently defined, and the recurrence of this fragment of G flat has an obvious enough meaning in the context. The second main C major unit, however—Sachs' 'Verachtet mir die Meister nicht' —is a clearly formed home—bright—dark—home structure to which the ominous dark-side music of his 'Habt Acht!' acts as a coda returning to C major with the 'Nürnberg' music. The chorus's 'Ehrt eure deutschen Meister' concludes both this structure and that of the whole work.

Act III is crowded with interlocking structures, some of which have already been referred to. First of all, if we regard the main G major structure (from the prelude up to Eva's and Sachs' endearments) as extended to include the music from 'Wach auf!' to 'Heil!', it interlocks with the main C major structure at the end of the work. The C major extending from the first verse to the last of the prize-song interlocks with the E flat of the conversation between Sachs and Walther. This E flat itself interlocks with the subsequent D major music by forming its tonal episodes. And the B♭ G of Sachs and Eva after the third verse of the Prize-song interlocks with the other keys in the first part of Act III by referring back to the appearances of B♭ G which form the structural outline of Act II. Sachs' B flat just referred to and the brief but decisive return to B flat after the G major endearments of Sachs and Eva create an interlocking structure with the end of the main C major structure of the act; and this B flat structure forms in turn the first element of the introduction to the final C major structure, finishing with the dance of the apprentices.

The beginning of the final C major structure, occurring at the entry of the Mastersingers, has already been foreshadowed by Sachs' 'Eine Meisterweise', and from that point to the entry of the Mastersingers may be considered an introduction to the main C major structure, interlocking with the B flat structure. The C major entry of the Mastersingers interlocks with the G major structure which follows it (beginning 'Wach auf!'), forming a small C major structure ending with the repetition of 'Heil!' The considerable extent of C major in which the Mastersingers criticise Beckmesser's song may be considered a further interlocking of this same structure.

Subsidiary threads in this act are represented by D major (first David with Sachs and later Beckmesser), referring back to the use of that key for David's conversation with Walther and 'Am stillen Herd' in the first act. The same key reappears at

Sachs' 'Ein Kind ward hier geboren', in the course of the B flat
structure immediately preceding the final C major structure, and
forming a bridge between B flat and the C major which begins
(at 'Eine Meisterweise') the introduction to that structure; again,
briefly, after Sachs' minor key 'Euch macht ihr's leicht' and
before his main subsequent G major structure begins; and
lastly when Walther comes forward to sing his contest song—the
connection with the subsidiary thread explaining the otherwise
irrelevant use of D major for the *Abgesang* (just as the thread
of E major had provided the explanation for the use of that key
in the prelude), and referring the mind back to Walther's previous 'preliminary' key of D, for 'Am stillen Herd'. It is worth
noticing, though here it is more an ornamental factor than in
the B♭ G case in Acts II and III, that in three of the five cases
in this act D major is followed by C major, creating one of the
characteristic two-key units of tonality to which we have previously referred. We may also note that in this opera the second
of the two keys is in each case one of the primary keys of the
opera: B♭G—BF—DC.

B major, as distinct from the two-key unit BF (which is part
of an overall interlocking structure yet to be considered),
creates a less frequent but very marked subsidiary thread in
the course of the opera, and its appearances in this act are,
first, in the course of Sachs' soliloquy after David goes out, and
later at the beginning of the process of modulation which
accompanies the transformation of scenes. (Wagner's use of
keys with special, subjective meaning needs separate discussion.
B major seems to imply for him various sorts of purity.)

C major, as well as being the basic key of the whole work,
runs persistently as a subsidiary thread through this act: at the
end of Sachs' first soliloquy, for the first verses of the prize-
song, at the end of Sachs' comment on Beckmesser before his
conversation with Eva, for the third verse of the song (forming
a C major interlocking structure with the earlier verses as its
beginning), at Sachs' 'Eine Meisterweise' which is the beginning
of the introduction to the final C major structure, as a subsidiary

key in the music of the guilds, and for the Mastersingers' comment on Beckmesser's version of the prize-song.

E flat is of notable importance at the beginning of the act, where, as has already been pointed out, it not only forms the main key of a tonal unit when Walther and Sachs are in conversation but continues as the subsidiary key of the following tonal unit on D; we then hear no more of it until Beckmesser mounts the mound, where it forms the middle section of a C major unit.

F major is one of the three primary keys of the opera, and like the other primary keys, also acts as a subsidiary thread. In this act its first appearance has more importance than the diagram conveys, because it is expressed by means of the 'Nürnberg' tune which at every appearance has a strong structural effect. The second appearance of F major, at the entry of the guilds, either is, or refers pointedly to, one of the fundamental structural factors of the opera, as will be shown. The last appearances of this key are, first, as an ornamental factor—yet still inevitably relating to the subsidiary thread—when Pogner offers Walther the chain, and finally as one of the structural factors in the smaller-scale C major structure of Sachs' 'Verachtet mir die Meister nicht'.

The key of A flat, though its main function in this act is the specific one of referring back to the corresponding tonality of the former conversation between Sachs and Eva in Act II, yet appears twice more in modulatory passages.

The tonal thread of B flat is continued in this act, first as the second element of the E flat structure of the conversation between Sachs and Walther and then in the sizeable B flat structure, beginning as Sachs covers the emotions of Walther and Eva after the third verse of the song and ending with the apprentices' dance.

G major continues, first as the second subsidiary section of the E flat structure just mentioned, then as the second key of the two-key unit B♭ G after the third verse of the song, and finally as the second structural element in Sachs' 'Verachtet

Meistersinger, Act III

Main Tonalities	Interlocking				Subsidiary						

```
Main
Tonalities   Interlocking        Subsidiary
   G            G                    G
   D                                   D
                                                    B
                    Eb                    Eb
                         C                     C
   D                     C                D      C
   Ab                    C                       C
   Bb                         Bb                      Bb
   G            G                    G            Bb
                              Bb                 D
   C                     C                     C
                                                    B              (Gb)
                                                    E
                                             A
   C                     C                     C            F
   F            F                             C
                                              C        A mi
                                                       A mi
   F            F                             C                 F
                         Bb                        Bb
   C            G        C                G   C
   C            G        C                     C       A mi
                                          D
   C            G        C                G   C
   C                 Eb  C                Eb  C
                         C                     C       E mi
                                              C        E mi
                                              C        E ma
                              D                C
   C                     C                     C       A mi
                                              C
   C            F        C                     C       E mi
   C            G    Eb  C                G    C            (Gb)
                F        C                     C
   C                     C                     C            F
   chrom                 C                     C
   coda                  C                     C
   C                     C                     C
```

mir die Meister nicht'. (Its appearances at 'Wach auf!' and Sachs' 'Wenn ihr die Kunst so hoch schon ehrt' are part of a more important structure, but they are also part of the subsidiary G major thread.)

The key of E, major or minor, is represented in this act first as part of Sachs' soliloquy after David goes out, next (though very unobtrusively and probably inconsiderably) as part of the process of modulation as the shop changes into the meadow, and finally, as E minor, for Beckmesser's song, altering to E major as Sachs assures the listeners of the poem's validity. (See page 67.)

The tonal categories applied to the opera as a whole give the following result. (The subsidiary threads are omitted because, overall, they are so numerous as to be incomprehensible.)

Main Tonalities	Interlocking Tonalities		Act	Scene
C	C		Prelude	
‖		B♭		
C	C		I	1
F		F		3
‖	C			
F		F		
G		F	G — Prelude, II	1
‖			A♭	4
G			G	7
G			Prelude, III	1
‖			A♭	4
G				4
[F	F			5
F]		F		
	B♭			
C				
‖				
C				

We postulated that the structural framework of Wagner's richly ornamented edifice must be simple and massive, and the 'main tonalities' column of this diagram gives us our demonstration: C F G (F) C.

We should not be justified in omitting reference to the penultimate key of F, for it occurs in the nature of a digression when a long process of dominant suspense in C has prepared the mind for the final entry of the main key. Yet it would be a mistake to take the mirror characteristic it produces very seriously. For the F major music of the guilds is only four or five minutes long and spends a lot of its time in the dominant and the mediant minor. We can be content to regard the overall structure of the work as that most durable of tonal procedures: home—second tonality—section of opposite tonal relation— home, expressed in this case as home—dark—bright—home.

Although in the diagram the G major which constitutes the whole of Act II looks longer than the G major section of Act III, in fact it is the other way round; and that these framework sections are of comparable weight is shown by their approximate duration: C major, 25 minutes; F major, 45 minutes; G major (Act II), 60 minutes; G major (Act III), 75 minutes; C major, 35 minutes. The proportions of classical movements in sonata form vary widely, but in general it is true to assert that the second main tonal area is longer than the first, and to postulate without reference to particular examples that the length of the final material in the tonic would not need to be restricted as long as it was of sufficient length to fulfil the structural requirement. This 'structural requirement', taken over the whole work, is that the first tonality must be satisfactorily established, and this can if the composer wishes be done briefly since its primary position gives it also primacy. The second tonality must be satisfactorily established, and this, unless the composer has unusually epigrammatic purposes in hand, will take longer. The process of tonal opposition must follow, and this can be long or short, determinate or indeterminate *in general*, as long as there is somewhere—usually soon after the start—a decisive assertion of the sensation of tonal opposition. Finally the home tonality must return and be consolidated: a process which in fully developed movements will not be very short but need not be confined in length to any very strictly stated proportion of the whole. In these general terms, the proportions of the tonal areas in *Die Meistersinger* are acceptably related as 2 : 4 : 11 : 3 compared, for example, to the 2 : 4 : 8 : 6 (plus 6 for the coda) in the first movement of the Ninth Symphony.

Finally we may note that *Parsifal*, similarly analysed, exhibits the same procedure of opposite tonal relation within an enclosing tonality. Its overall structure is A♭ C/B minor B flat minor / A♭, in which C major is on the bright side of A flat and both B minor and B flat minor on the dark side of C. They are also on the dark side of A flat. For the purpose of the tonal opposition, this would not have been necessary, since there is plenty of space between C (which is as bright as you can get in relation to A flat) and A flat. But we shall see Beethoven also choosing to put his section of opposite tonal relation on the dark side of the tonic as well as of the bright second tonality, even when it was not necessary. The procedure produces not only the sensation of tonal opposition but—as also, but then inevitably, occurs when the tonic is major and the second main tonality the dominant major—in addition the sensation of what we may call 'counterpoise' of the bright and dark side areas in relation to the tonic.

Tristan und Isolde differs, in that it consists of two huge interlocking structures:

C	A♭B	C	A♭B
(the whole of Act I,	(climax of	(arrival of	(Isolde's
including important	Act II)	Isolde's ship)	*Liebestod*)
parts of the prelude;			
and Act II to the			
arrival of Tristan)			

From the point of view of the relation between the musical structure and the narrative it is instructive to note that, just as the two C minor elements in the *St Matthew Passion* are textually concerned with 'watching-over', so in *Tristan* the three defining areas of C major are all 'arrivals': the end of Act I (the previous parts of that Act having been in a highly chromaticised C minor) the arrival in Cornwall; in Act II, Tristan's arrival at Isolde's garden; in Act III, Isolde's arrival at Kareol. The identity of the love-music in A♭B at the ends of Acts II and III, constituting the closed structure interlocking with C, needs no stressing.

POST-WAGNERIAN OPERA

VERDI

If we expected Beethoven's single opera to depart from the tradition of the trade, at least a failure on his part to do so could have been explained away by the fact that he was a classical structuralist. The music of Verdi is surely the place above all where Romantic passion would be expected to scatter tonal structure to the winds. Yet it is not so.

Of Verdi's operas, those that have held the stage more firmly than any others are not merely clear-cut tonal structures in their essence, but follow the traditional procedure of interlocking structures without exception, until he reaches *Falstaff*. There, perhaps because he is writing a comedy, he follows the procedures of Mozart's and Wagner's comedies and creates a closed C major structure. The first two acts themselves constitute a closed structure of C, the first part of Act III is a largely modulating section, and the final section of the opera precedes its return to C with a large-scale structure on the dominant.

Il Trovatore interlocks E major-to-minor, which encloses A flat minor-to-major, with E flat minor, which encloses D flat minor-to-major interlocking with C major-to-minor which encloses F. (This is a characteristic predilection of Verdi's for transferring keys from one mode to the other.) *Rigoletto* interlocks a double-tonality-unit of A flat/C (mostly minor) with D flat major-to-minor. *Aida* interlocks D major-to-minor with a tonality of D flat which may either be considered a double-tonality-unit of F sharp (G flat)/D flat in a reversing-end structure or simply D flat major-to-minor, in which case the final tonality of G flat remains dramatically appropriate as a further move to the dark side, expressing, with a naïveté of direct impressionism no more striking than some of Bach's, the gloom of its final scene.

There might seem to be an objection to the opera ending in a key other than that of the second main interlocking tonality. But as long as the main tonalities of the work are clear there would be no more objection to a dramatically (or otherwise) comprehensible 'postlude' in another key than there is to the frequently used procedure of putting the prelude in a key other than either or any of the main ones. Furthermore, Verdi precedes the D flat procedure of Amonasro's conversation with Aida with (admittedly at some distance) two well-defined descents to G flat referring to the status of prisoners. These may be thought acceptable as the materials of a rather long-arched reversing-end process in which what is indecisive tonally, because of the small-scale and long-distance character of its start, is rendered comprehensible by its dramatic relevance.

RICHARD STRAUSS

Similarly, *Der Rosenkavalier* is an interlocking structure of E major, running from the overture to the Waltz in Act III—after a decisive return to finish Act II—and G major, which begins with the start of Act II—after a preliminary appearance in its minor mode at the Marschallin's 'Die Zeit'—and ends with the two appearances of the duet between Sophie and Octavian at the end of the opera.

We may note that all but two of Strauss's operas (*Salome* and *Die ägyptische Helena*) end away from the tonality in which they start. *Salome's* bloody coda indeed brings the opera literally to an end in C minor, but this is clearly a narrative, not a structural use of tonality. All the tone-poems are closed structures. *Also sprach Zarathustra* is not an exception to this, though the suggestion has sometimes been made that it is. It spends much of its time moving from B to C (lower leading-note to

tonic) and back—three times before reaching the closing
Ziemlich langsam that completes the C structure with which it
began. The *Nachtwandlerlied* is still, though chromatic, on C, and
there follows a B major coda which continues—and carries to
an extreme—the classical tradition of ornamental key-change
in a coda. After this the original tonality of C—which has been
structurally completed *before* the coda—returns by means of

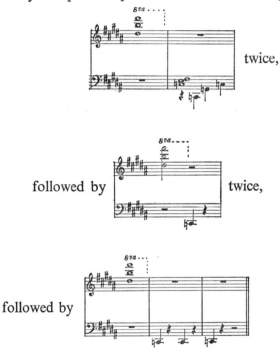

twice,

followed by ... twice,

followed by

Sleight-of-hand in the manner of Beethoven, and in this case
ornamental.

PART II

A Theory of Tonality in
Instrumental Music

PART II

A Theory of Tonality in Instrumental Music

BAROQUE AND CLASSICAL STRUCTURES

Classical Sonata-form

The structure of instrumental music in the major-minor period, apart from ostinato procedures such as ground-basses, is dominated throughout by tonality. This statement is in principle generally accepted, but its acceptance is vitiated by failure to apply the principle in two important areas. First, a good many structures of considerable importance are treated as though they were dominated by the thematic structure; and secondly, even within structures admitted to be tonally dominated, some areas of such structures are discussed in primarily thematic terms, or in tonal terms faultily expressed. So that, in the first group, fugues, *rondeaux*, rondos and baroque concertos are rarely treated consistently as tonal structures; and in the second, in structures said to be dependent on inter-relationship of tonalities, only two tonal areas are considerably discussed.

We are now clearly on the verge of classical sonata-form, which will indeed serve as the basis of much of the following discussion. But it is not only sonata-form itself which suffers from incomplete tonal statement in most analyses, but its predecessors in the dance-forms of the Baroque period.

I choose deliberately as an example of this general failure to recognise the tonal reality of sonata-form and its relatives one of the best of present-day writers on the analysis of music, Peter Wishart, whose book called *Harmony* (which is mostly about tonality) is endearingly dedicated to one 'who also believes in studying real music'. It is therefore all the more surprising to find in it a classically incorrect statement of the nature of what is traditionally called the 'development section' of classical sonata-form. Mr Wishart says: ' . . . Its sole purpose is to obliterate the sensation of the tonic by means of a confusion of keys, so that the return of the tonic may have its appropriate effect of triumph.' All credit to Mr Wishart for observing that what is concerned is the return *of the tonic*, not of the first tune of the movement. But otherwise his statement, though true of the cases in which it applies, does not apply to a good many examples of what would unquestionably be generally accepted as sonata-form. It cannot therefore constitute a generalisation about this structure.

The fact is that soon after the emergence of major-minor tonality from the establishment of the sensation of a 'leading-note' led to the process of merging of the modes, the inter-relationships of keys began to express themselves as processes of tonal opposition. That is to say, it began to be recognised that keys are related not only as dominants and subdominants, supertonics and submediants of each other, but also in an audible sense as relatively 'bright' or 'dark' (see page 20).

The structural effect of this discovery was that movements began to be devised with the specific intention of creating such 'processes of tonal opposition' as a consistent means of expression. We find it in full force in the music of Lully (I do not necessarily claim for him priority in the use of it: this sort of thing is usually 'in the air' rather than the invention of any one composer), and more casually in the brass music of Pezel. Any number of examples by any number of composers could, in fact, by diligence be brought forward.

In the late Baroque dance-forms which are the fore-runners of Classical sonata-form this principle of opposite tonal relation is in constant (though of course not exclusive) use, and the greatest composers of the period were surprisingly and instructively unconcerned to express any originality in their use of it. Thus we find the great Bach, in—for example—the C major Suite for Orchestra, using the procedure |:C—G:|:A minor or D minor or both and back to C:| without exception through the whole series of nine dance-movements, except that the second Bourrée moves to the dominant *chord* instead of the dominant key, at the end of the first structural element. In terms of the relationships established on page 20, G is on the bright side of C and A minor and D minor are on the dark side of G (and of C for that matter, but that is not the principle of the structure— see below on this page).

Thematically, as is characteristic at this period, this essentially tonal structure is expressed without 'dramatisation'—to use Tovey's phrase—of the tonal changes.

In the Classical period, in contrast to this unemphatic thematic execution of the tonal design, tonality itself becomes not only the dominant structural function but, by reason of its more 'dramatic' thematic presentation, a primary means of expression. In particular, it provides the only generalisation valid in all cases for the overall structure of sonata-form. For Classical sonata-form is defined not by a series of thematic procedures, but by a series of tonal areas in specific relation to one another:

(1) *A first main tonal area*, usually expressed by means of a striking thematic factor, though not necessarily or even probably by a large-scale 'Romantic'-style tune.

(2) Movement to and establishment of a *second main tonal area*.

(3) *A third main tonal area* whose relation to the second will be the opposite of that obtaining between the second and the first (i.e., if the second is on the bright side of the first the third will be on the dark side of the second, and *vice versa*).

(4) *A return*, structurally thereafter unweakened, to the first tonality.

The movement to the second tonal area may be abrupt or

leisurely, and in either case distinct or indistinct. The tonality which is to serve in this structural capacity may be abruptly established immediately after the announcement of the first theme in the tonic, only to be put in question by a series of modulations followed by a return, more or less distinctly achieved, to the second tonality. In some cases it is impossible to decide whether the first or the second establishment of the second tonality is the structural one, and in such cases the composer obviously intended the ambiguity. The caution of our definition is thus justified: *movement to and establishment of a second main tonal area.* Any generalisation which attempts to become more specific, as to either the moment or the means of transfer to the second tonality, will become false. On the other hand, a leisurely transition from the first key to the second may make it quite clear at what moment the change has occurred.

The second main tonality, if the moment of its start is sufficiently clear to allow its length to be measured, is usually established at greater length than the first tonality. But there are many cases in the works of both Haydn and Beethoven in which the music, after the assertion of the first tonality, merely 'drifts' into the second main tonality, leaving it to the listener to become gradually aware that the change has occurred and is not going to be reversed.

The third main tonal area can be expressed either by means of one key only, led to and left by brief modulatory procedures, as in the first movement of Mozart's A major Piano Concerto, K. 414; or, more characteristically, by a series of key changes, all of which, unless they are for 'surprise' purposes such as will be discussed, will be in the 'appropriate' tonal relation to the second main tonal area (i.e., usually on its dark side). Thematically it may be a process of development of previously stated material—its own material having the character not of statement but of manipulation of previous statements. Or it may consist of procedures based on thematic material (in Mozart often of a formula sort) not previously heard in the movement.

There is however in general use among both Baroque and

Classical composers another kind of opposition of tonal relation. It is characteristically used when the minor dominant acts as second main tonal area to a minor tonic. Minor keys being ambiguous in relation to one another, it is not easy to produce a clearly defined sensation of tonal opposition between any three of them (e.g., tonic–dominant, dominant–subdominant: relationships whose inter-relationship in the major mode would be unquestionable).

Beethoven, it should be noted, does use this inter-relationship of minors, overcoming the possibility of ambiguity in a number of ways. In the last movement of the piano sonata Op. 27 (the 'Moonlight') the keys concerned are C sharp minor—G sharp minor, with the subdominant relationship of F sharp minor (sounding more than ordinarily dark because it is preceded by the chord of C sharp as the tonic major) occupying nearly the whole of the third main tonal area. In the first movement of the D minor piano sonata, Op. 31 No. 2, the keys are D minor—A minor, with the more distant key of F sharp minor, the relative minor of the dominant major, taking most of the third tonal area. Here the required darkness of relationship is achieved by its being preceded by the chord of F sharp major. In the rondo of the same sonata however, it is achieved by the simple process of starting in the tonic D minor and adding successive movements on what would for major keys be unquestionably the dark side until, even among minors, the ear is convinced.

But the normal procedure adopted to produce the sensation of opposite tonal relation when a minor tonic has been followed by the minor dominant is to oppose the minor-to-minor relationship of the first two tonal areas with a minor-to-major relationship between the second and the third. The sensation is extraordinarily bright and 'masculine' after the ambiguity of the two minors, and its validity as a type of tonal opposition needs only the authority of the ear.

The structural return to the tonic may be achieved by any thematic means the composer likes. This is very often, though it need not be, the re-appearance of the opening material of the first main tonal area. That it need not re-appear should not need emphasis. But students of music in particular are likely to suppose that it must, because the traditional terms which purport to describe the elements of sonata-form, and which are unfortunately still in general use, are almost totally irrelevant, as generalisations, to the musical facts.

The term 'first subject' is not without significance in the context, in that the opening material of a movement such as this is usually clear-cut and decisive. It is objectionable only insofar as it implies that there will be a second subject.

The term 'transition' is also not without significance. There sometimes is one. But it carries two implications which easily lead to misunderstanding: that the transition will be of at least definable length, and that its purpose will be to proceed in an unsurprising fashion from the first material to the second. (The traditional usage means from the first *subject* to the second. In reality, if it exists at all, it leads from the first *tonal area* to the second.) Neither implication is necessarily valid. Both Mozart and Beethoven use a procedure in which the second main tonality is introduced decisively and without transitional material, immediately following the establishment of the first tonality. Thus there need be no transition at all. As to 'proceeding in an unsurprising fashion': if there *is* a transition, and if the expression 'proceeding in an unsurprising fashion' is recognised as applying to such a situation as occurs in Beethoven's Fifth Symphony (Ex. 1), where it consists merely of:

Ex. 1

BEETHOVEN: Symphony No. 5 in C minor - 1st movement

the last two chords of an element which has appeared to belong to the first main tonal area and four notes that follow, then it is relevant. But then the word 'transition' has changed its meaning from 'a structural area of transition' to 'a transitional procedure' too short for the concept of a structural area to be applied to it. Given such large areas of inapplicability, it is better to do without the term 'transition' as a generalisation about classical sonata-form, and use it only in the particular cases to which it applies.

The 'second subject', as a generalisation, is a figment of analytical imagination. There may be clearly defined thematic material, with a definable moment of commencement, expressing the second main tonality, or there may not. We shall discuss shortly what happens if there is not.

The word 'codetta', often applied to the end materials of any section of a movement (other than the last section: the 'coda'), is generally undesirable. Its effect is nearly always to imply something much more clear-cut and decisive than is actually present in the music. In all kinds of music there are many extensions of preceding material to a cadence. But to call it that—an extension to a cadence—is generally more useful than the use of a 'name' word which may mislead by appearing to create a structurally 'required' entity. For such an entity, if at first it cannot be located, must be sought, and if not found, then invented.

The term 'development' is satisfactory on the condition that 'the possibilities of previously announced thematic material are being exploited' (Westrup and Harrison). But two things should be emphasised about it. First, that in music you can only develop thematic material. Individual tonalities are either present or not present (i.e., the music can be in them or out of them) but they cannot develop. Second, that you cannot develop what is not yet there: the thematic material being developed must have been previously announced. Of course there is nothing to prevent the emergence from complex material of a simpler version of itself —for example, Brahms' 'skeletonising' process in re-statements of themes. But to regard this as a process of development-in-reverse, the earlier material constituting what, *if it had appeared after it*, would have been a development of the later material, is itself a recognition of the normal order. Walking backwards is a perfectly feasible procedure, which soldiers and dancers are taught to do. But 'walking', unqualified, means walking forward.

There are many movements generally accepted as being in classical sonata-form in which the third main tonal area is expressed in previously unused, often formula-like material. They cannot be said to have a 'development' section, since nothing is being developed: something new is happening. If they are not to be regarded as being in sonata-form for this reason, the meaning of that term is being restricted to a much smaller area of application than traditional usage appears to intend. Clearly, in terms of the intention of traditional usage, they *are* in sonata-form; the phrase 'development section' as applied to this type of structure, is thus shown to be sometimes false. As a generalisation therefore it is shown to be misleading.

The term 'recapitulation' is perhaps the most vexatious of all these falsehoods masquerading as descriptions. For the word in its normally accepted use means to go back to the beginning and say what you said before, if not precisely as you said it before, at any rate with the same meaning as before.

In contrast with this, what happens at the return of the first key in a musical structure of this sort *may be*, and very likely will be to a considerable extent, a return of the material with which the movement opened. But when this material was first used its function was to express *both* of the two tonal areas which constitute the first structural element of the movement: and insofar as the word 'meaning' can be applied to a musical structure this function of expressing the two tonalities as pillars of the tonal structure is one of its most important meanings. When it returns after the third main tonal area its function is precisely opposite: it *must not* move from the first to any other tonality of structural significance, because if it does there seems no reason why the movement should ever come to an end— unless, of course, subsequent events demonstrate that the structure never was that of sonata-form but something much more extended. Thus one of its chief 'meanings' on its first appearance must *not* occur on its second, and furthermore its content may be so radically changed that it may seem arbitrary to refer to it as the same material at all.

Then why call it a 'recapitulation'? It is more usefully described as the structural return of the first tonality, expressed usually by means of some, all or nearly all of the thematic material which had originally constituted the first and second main tonal areas, and sometimes by means which differ very considerably from that material. Especially we should guard against assuming that the structural return to the first key will be expressed by a re-appearance of the opening material of the movement *from the beginning*. The classical composer never undertook to do any such thing, even though he often does.

The generalisations about the nature of sonata-form given on pages 79-84 are invariable in their application (that is to say that if a movement does not fulfil these requirements it is not in sonata-form, or can only be said to be so by association), and they are all tonal. The statement is not arbitrary. It is devised to express the facts presented by the material: we are not asking the material to conform to the definition.

With the generalisations established, we can proceed to the individuality of the Classical composers who used this structure more than any other: individualities expressed chiefly through thematic treatment.

HAYDN

The most strongly characteristic feature of Haydn's symphonic handling of sonata-form is his process of allowing formula-like material to 'drift' from the first tonality to the second in such a way that the second is established mainly by persistence after an unobtrusive arrival. The movement, whether or not it is preceded by a slow introduction (usually thematically independent), will have started, characteristically, with either a loud vigorous tune or a soft, sprightly one. The latter is very often the kind known as 'self-repeating': its second half repeating its first, with sometimes the first ending on the dominant chord and the second altered to come to the tonic.

Ex. 2

HAYDN: Symphony No. 103 in Eb - 1st movement

In the case shown it is repeated unaltered.

The subsequent formula process may start with references to this opening tune (or it may not), and such references may recur towards the end of the formula-process, which by that time will have established the second main tonality. Both these procedures are used in the first movement of the 103rd Symphony. Or the formula-process may lead undramatically to the second tonality, signal that something new is about to happen, and start off afresh. This fresh start will open either with more formula, or with a statement of the opening tune of the first tonality, transferred to the second, or with a short tune which undoubtedly recalls Mozart's method: that of establishing the second main tonality with something that can properly be called a 'second subject', or group of subjects.

It would be misleading to apply either of those terms to Haydn's procedures here, even when they occur at all, because they have too casual a character to bear so much structural weight. One has the impression, even in such a movement, that formula would have done just as well—as in fact it does in many movements of Haydn's—but that he chose to insert a fragment of more decisive melody, perhaps consciously in recognition of Mozart's characteristic procedure. Alternatively, there may be nothing of such melodic character to establish a moment at which the second main tonality may be said to start. In such a case there will be no such moment definable.

But Haydn sometimes chooses to introduce a tune, as distinct from the formula procedure we have been discussing, towards the end of the formula section and of the second main tonal area. It too, because of its position and its generally whimsical character, is unsuited to fulfilling the structurally unnecessary function of a second subject.

Ex. 3

HAYDN: Symphony No. 103 in E♭ - 1st movement

p

MOZART

Mozart was more inclined to unfold a series of quite small tunes, many of them repeated as well as being self-repeating, and all of them taken together constituting a sizeable procedure. Those in the first tonality *may* be somewhat larger and more masculine in character than those in the second. This is presumably the basis of the traditional fondness for describing Classical sonata procedure in general as involving a 'masculine' thematic quality in what is called the 'first subject' and a more 'lyrical' quality in what is called the second, though neither the masculinity nor the lyricism nor the firstness nor the secondness —except in the analytically irrelevant sense of mere time-sequence—can be depended upon to occur.

A typical example is the C major Symphony, K. 425 (the *Linz*). The 15 tune-fragments of its first and second main tonal areas demonstrate not only the validity of the above statements, but also the impossibility of making a thematic generalisation about classical sonata-form applicable to both Mozart and Haydn.

As we have noted, Mozart and Beethoven have in common with each other, but not with Haydn, a liking for modulating abruptly to the key which is to become that of the second main tonal area, immediately after the statement of the single theme likely to constitute the whole of the first tonal area. After this the music may continue to modulate considerably, before settling down into what (from its mere position in time combined with its being the same key as had previously been abruptly established), can only be regarded as the second main tonal area; and the question whether that area started after the modulating process or at the first plunge is left unanswered, unanswerable and unimportant. This is the procedure in Mozart's 'small' G minor Symphony, K. 183, and in Beethoven's Fifth Symphony. The latter, like most nonconformist structures created by acceptedly 'great' composers, is generally treated, with a reverence appropriate to its greatness, as conformist. But it conforms to Beethoven's characteristic procedures, not to the traditional description of them. Mozart's procedure in K. 183 is:

Ex. 4

MOZART: Symphony in G minor, K.183 - 1st movement

as the first 'plunge' to B flat, followed by:

Ex. 5

Beethoven's sleight-of-hand transfer to the relative major in the first movement of the Fifth Symphony is shown in Example 1 on page 82.

BEETHOVEN

Besides agreeing with Mozart in this 'plunge-and-smoke-screen' way of establishing the second main tonality, Beethoven also agrees with Haydn's approach to it, though his way of doing so is his own. This way-of-his-own is the process of starting with a well-defined theme in the home key, and following it with music which drifts off to the second main tonality in such a way that it becomes meaningless to assert any one moment as the moment of structural change.

In the first movement of the Third Symphony, for example, the possibilities are these (Ex. 6):

Ex. 6

BEETHOVEN: Symphony No. 3 in E♭ - 1st movement

and whichever you choose you will feel you are short-changing the others. The answer is, not to attempt to choose, since Beethoven clearly intended the ambiguity.

But there is no ambiguity about the establishment of the second main tonality itself. We remain uncertain as to which modulations to the dominant were structural and which ornamental, but we have no doubt at all, that by the time we reach the end of the first structural element the key of the dominant has been very firmly established.

Beethoven's third main tonal area—the section of opposite tonal relation—quite often contains 'surprise' appearances of keys in an 'inappropriate' relationship to the preceding tonal area. He was not the first to use this sort of procedure. Haydn had used similar processes of surprise but, as in the first movement of the 102nd Symphony, created it in the middle of the dark-side material, recalling Bach's characteristic bright-side interruptions in dark middle areas (Ex. 7):

Ex. 7

HAYDN: Symphony No. 102 in B♭ - 1st movement

Beethoven's preference, shown for example in the first movements of the E flat symphony and the E flat piano concerto, is to 'frame' the actual section of opposite tonal relation in a key very strongly on the bright side of the second main tonal area, instead of on its dark side. In the symphony, the bright key chosen is C major, the supertonic major of the second main key, thematically expressed in the material of the first of the 'possibilities' to be regarded as establishing the second main tonality (Ex. 8).

Ex. 8

It leads abruptly, as such 'surprise' interruptions usually do, to its own minor for the start of the process of tonal opposition.

On its return the bright key is thematically expressed in the main theme of the movement, which thus takes on the character of a 'false return' (Ex. 9).

Ex. 9

BEETHOVEN: Symphony No. 3 in E♭ - 1st movement

In the E flat concerto the bright key is G—the submediant major of the second main key. Both before and after the process of tonal opposition it is thematically expressed by the same tune, the last of a series in the orchestral statement of themes. The second G major appearance of this tune, played by the piano after the section of opposite tonal relation, is short, but its thematic character and its relative tonality are so striking as to make its 'framing' character unmistakable.

First G major appearance:

Ex. 10
BEETHOVEN: Piano Concerto No. 5 in E♭ - 1st movement

Surprising as it is—and remains—in its contexts, there is nothing structurally upsetting about the device of 'framing' the process of tonal opposition in keys that contradict it. In it, Beethoven expresses again his preference for a tonal scheme more expanded *ornamentally*—not structurally—than that which had served his predecessors. Similar procedures, expressing the same preference, are the tendency towards modulation within a tonal area and the use of a second main tonality other than the dominant after a major tonic and other than the relative major after a minor one.

A less basic, but still characteristic tonal procedure is his liking for modulation as it were by sleight-of-hand: the effrontery of proceeding chromatically by half-step to the tonic of the new key—often by single notes unharmonised—and pretending it has been established. For example, the move to the structural key-change in the orchestral statements of themes in the first and second piano concertos, and the return to the open fifth on A after the B flat area of the first movement in the Ninth Symphony.

Such a move is unexpected, and the unexpected has an aspect of the incongruous, and the incongruous is a basic element in humour. So it is not surprising to find that tonality itself is one of Beethoven's chief means of humorous expression, as the scherzo of the Third Symphony shows.

Its initial E flat material sounds introductory, and as a result the sensation of the first main tonal area is brought about by means of the tune in B flat—the first thing you could seriously call a 'tune' in the movement—which is actually the material of the *second* main tonal area. The third main tonal area opens with further introductory material modulating chromatically to the bright key of F major, in which the tune previously heard in B flat returns. Thence to the dark-side key of G minor—a process of opposite tonal relation (vis-à-vis B and F) *within* the second main structural element—after which 'the tune' returns in what we understood to be the first main key: B flat. Thus, when the tune wrenches melodically upward and tonally downward into the real first key of E flat it achieves not only the uproarious character of the transfer itself, but also the thump between the shoulder-blades as Beethoven shouts at us that we have been tricked. Not every conductor of this work seems to be aware that he has been tricked.

Ex. 11

BEETHOVEN: Symphony No. 3 in E♭ - 3rd movement
(a) Introductory material: *(b) 'The tune':*

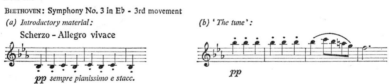

Beethoven's characteristic large-scale coda usually, but not always, contains a considerable area of tonal change. It may occur either at the beginning (the more usual method) or at the end (as in the last movement of the C sharp minor quartet, Op. 131), and may be on either the dark or the bright side of the tonic, with a tendency to the former.

It may be well here to set at rest—if it still walks—the ghost of a controversy. Passions used to be aroused by the question whether sonata-form should be considered a two-part or a three-part form: a question which derives, like so many other confusions, from failure to recognise the essentially tonal nature of the structure.

That it is essentially two-part is shown by its frequent repetition of 'both' its parts, and this two-partness is tonal: two tonal areas forming the first structural element and two tonal areas the second structural element, with the second tonal area of the second element the same as the first tonal area of the first element. But no-one would deny that, superimposed on this tonal two-partness, there tends to be a three-part thematic plan consisting of (1) two statements of two sets of material (not necessarily distinct enough from each other to be called first and second 'subjects', or even 'groups of subjects', divided on their first appearance between the first two main tonalities and making their second appearance both in the home tonality; and (2) material, either free or developmental, intervening between the two statements.

The relationship between the tonal two-partness and the thematic three-partness can be diagrammed as:

First structural element (two tonal areas)	*Superimposed thematic structure*
(1) First main tonal area	A
(2) Second main tonal area	B (which may be based on A)

Second structural element (two tonal areas)	
(1) Section of opposite tonal relation	Development or free material
(2) Structural return to the home key	A B

With the nature and the pervasive character of tonal structure thus established, and before going on to consider other Classical and some Romantic uses of it, it is time to note the structural tonality of the Baroque forms mentioned earlier: the fugue, the rondeau and the concerto.

Fugue

J. S. Bach

The development of fugal procedures from those of the madrigal, though fascinating, is primarily a thematic matter until late in the seventeenth century. Though it is not without tonal interest, we are better advised to go—as usual—direct to the works of Bach.

His fugue has often been misrepresented, and from more than one point of view. Not only has it been presented as if its thematic procedures were all that mattered about it, and the more complicated you could make those seem the better; but insofar as its tonal scheme has been referred to at all it has been bowdlerised into the 'academic' fugue which came to monstrous birth —monstrous as a dead thing capable of reproducing its kind— some fifty years after Bach's death.

There are only two aspects of Bach's kind of fugue concerning which one can generalise: the exposition and the tonal plan. When the exposition is over anything at all can happen from a thematic point of view, and the only way to describe it is to say what does happen in this or that fugue.

The nature of fugal exposition has often been stated and, though academic unrealities still survive (such as solemn pondering over 'right' and 'wrong' answers), there is no need to set it out again in the present context. We can proceed at once to consideration of the tonal plan.

Apart from dance movements, Bach is particularly fond of some version of: home—a dark middle—home. This can be ornamented in any or all of three ways. (1) By returning to the tonic or the dominant or both in or about the middle of the dark section. (Haydn also follows this principle when, in the middle of the third main tonal area—essentially a dark-side area (see page 89)—in the first movement of the 102nd Symphony, he introduces a cheerfully irrelevant, very bright entry of the main tune in C major before dutifully returning to C minor to get on with the structure.) (2) By moving structurally to the dominant immediately after the completion of the first main tonal area—in which case the overall structure becomes a home —bright-side-of-home/dark-side-of-the-bright—home procedure. (3) By returning structurally to the dominant (or theoretically any key on the bright side of home) just before the final return to the tonic. In this case, if (2) has also been used, the overall structure becomes something in the nature of a tonal 'mirror'— a structural entity which we shall later need to go into at length.

If for convenience we use 'bright' to signify 'bright-side-of-home' and 'dark' to signify 'dark-side-of-the-bright', we can set out these possibilities as:

home		dark		dark		home	
home		dark	tonic or dominant or both	dark		home	
home	bright	dark		dark		home	
home	bright	dark	tonic or dominant or both	dark		home	
home	bright	dark		dark	bright	home	
home	bright	dark	tonic or dominant or both	dark	bright	home	

or more simply, using brackets to distinguish possibilities from necessities:

$$\text{home} \quad \text{(bright)} \quad \text{dark} \begin{cases} \text{tonic or} \\ \text{dominant} \\ \text{or both} \end{cases} \text{dark} \quad \text{(bright)} \quad \text{home}$$

The dark sections will not as a rule consist of one key only, though one key may predominate. More often there will be a number of keys all in the appropriate relation to the quality of the preceding section. If the tonic or dominant or both return in the course of the dark-side structural element, the dark sections on either side of them will not necessarily or even probably be represented by the same keys. Their functional identity resides in their relation of darkness to what has gone before. The first bright section, if present at all, is nearly always the dominant where the tonic is major, and the relative minor where the tonic is minor. If it is present, and if it is followed by uninterrupted dark-side material, the resulting structure is the home—bright—dark—home which characterises so much music in both the Baroque and Classical periods, and which is discussed in detail on pages 79–93.

DAS WOHLTEMPERIERTES KLAVIER
Since they are typical of the variety with which Bach uses his unifying tonal schemes, the first three fugues of the forty-eight will serve as examples for commentary.

No. 1 in C major

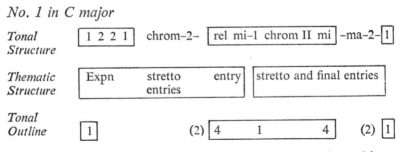

The whole movement consisting of entries of the subject, most of them in stretto, there is no need to do more than set out the tonal scheme. After the exposition, which has its tonic at both ends and two dominant entries between, there is a casual move, which may nonetheless be regarded as structural if the listener hears it so, to the dominant, and thence to a subject entry uncomplicated by stretto to a cadence in the relative minor. This appearance of the relative minor constitutes the beginning of the dark middle section which is continued and concluded by the move to the supertonic minor four bars later. In the meantime however there is an unusually decisive entry—the beginning of a series of stretto entries involving each of the four voices twice—in the tonic. We know by now that Bach is fond of brightening the dark side by a return to the tonic or the dominant or both (p. 95), but he does not usually do it by coming to a dark-side cadence and starting a new thematic section in the tonic. The result is the kind of 'cross-rhythm' between thematic and tonal factors which we can observe also in Beethoven (e.g., the trio in the second movement of the E flat String Quartet, Op. 127 (see pp. 156–8)).

Ex. 12

BACH: 48 Preludes and Fugues, No. 1 in C

(a) Subject

(b) Structural move to the dominant (bar 9)

(c) Structural move to the dark side (bar 11)

(d) Tonic 'interruption' of dark middle

(e) End of dark middle and beginning of structural appearance of the dominant

No. 2 in C minor

When the tonic is minor and the key of the 'answer' the dominant minor, the middle section, shown as 'dark' in the above diagrams, tends to become 'bright', often beginning with the relative major. It also can contain appearances of the subject in the tonic or the dominant or both, and since both will be minor the result is the reversal of the relations holding in the middle section when the subject is major. The process of answering the opening minor keys with the major middle exemplifies the process of tonal opposition special to minor tonics followed by minor dominants, described on page 81.

The fugue in C minor in Book 1 demonstrates these procedures.

The thematic processes of this fugue show the clarity-in-themselves combined with complexity-in-relationship characteristic of Bach's fugues. The three-part exposition separates its second and third entries with a strikingly chromatic sequential process, shown as 'X' in the diagram, and the whole process, shorn of its first entry and altered in detail, re-appears, again in the tonic, after an intervening procedure whose main function is the establishment of the 'bright' relative major expressed thematically by an entry of the subject. This entry is flanked on each side by a modulating process Y which thematically is basically the same each time. Thus, thematically, we have in outline: A : XA YAY AXA.

What follows is a version of Y—again 'bright' (the dominant of the relative major followed by the relative major) —and, after a process of dominant suspense based on A, an entry of A. Diagrammatic symmetry would now require a second appearance of Y. But Y was a modulating procedure and, since we are now at the end of the fugue it is replaced by a further entry, coda-like because it rests on a tonic pedal, of A.

The total thematic procedure |:A:| XA YAY AXA YAA creates several symmetries and suggestions of symmetries.

No. 2 in C minor

Tonal Structure:

1 mi 2 mi chrom 1 mi mod rel ma mod 1 mi–2 mi chrom 1 mi 2 of rel ma–rel ma–dom ch 1 dom susp 1

Thematic Structure:

| A A X | A | Y | A | Y¹ | A X ext | A | Y | on A | A ext |

Tonal Outline:

| 1 mi | | | | | | | | | 1 mi |

bright | dark | bright

are all realities of the situation. What is important is not to decide grimly and 'definitively' which is the 'correct' solution, but to recognise the shifting interrelation of all of them.

The tonal scheme is in 'cross-rhythm' with the thematic procedures, less decisively than that of the C major fugue, making its first structural move towards the end of the first Y and defining the new key most clearly at the following A. In the middle of the fugue the tonal and thematic schemes coincide. The bright dominant-of-the-relative-major, followed by the relative major itself, in the material Y which follows the middle tonic material, leads not to another bright entry, as the same material had done earlier, but back to the tonic. It might be argued that therefore it fails to fulfil the 'bright' requirement of the tonal scheme here put forward. But Baroque tonal

Ex. 13

BACH: 48 Preludes and Fugues, No. 2 in C minor

(a) Subject, shown as A

(b) Chromatic process, shown as X

(c) Modulating process, shown as Y

procedures are characteristically reserved compared to the more 'dramatic' Classical ones. The alternative here would be to assume that the structural return to the first tonality, as an end tonality, occurs after the first appearance of the relative major, and that the transient bright procedure at bar 23 is ornamental. The thematic similarity of the two bright sections argues against this, and even if the alternative were accepted it would leave the similarity—tonal and thematic—demanding some sort of recognition. Even a fleeting reference to a known procedure will achieve the result in the right context, and Bach and Beethoven, perhaps above all modern western composers, are masters of this art.

Beethoven

QUARTET IN C SHARP MINOR OP. 131

First Movement

Since the fugue is not one of the primary Classical forms we are not primarily concerned with its manifestations in that period. Yet we may pause long enough to note two things. First, that in fugues of any sort, even more than in most structures, the unifying function of tonality is especially important because of the probability of considerable thematic complexity. Second, that this truism is particularly applicable to Beethoven, who wrote his important fugues in his last period, using, most of all in the *Grosse Fuge*, a combination of rhythmic diversity and thematic reiteration which is apt to lead to analytical confusion unless order is restored through the recognition of tonality.

Beethoven, as the internal evidence of the work shows, was in no doubt about this. But most performers, despite the sensitivity characteristic of string quartet players, seem so to doubt whether the *Grosse Fuge* will hold together that they give most of their attention to ferocity. As a result, the music largely disappears and the listener attends to what is left of it with the solemnity due to a historic monument.

Its tonal design is in fact very simple:

Introduction B♭ G♭ | B♭ A♭ B♭ | reference to introduction B♭

The ternary middle section which the diagram makes clear is not only tonally ternary: the two B flat areas are thematically essentially the same. Thus we have tonally a rondo structure, with G flat on the dark side of the home key, a return to the tonic, and A flat on the bright side of G flat.

Ex. 14

BEETHOVEN: Grosse Fuge, op. 133

(a) B♭ area

(b) G♭ area

(c) middle-section B♭ areas

(d) A♭ area

The C sharp minor fugue of Op. 131 is equally straight-forward: not so in quality of thought, but as to the factors of tonal design which enable the listener to perform his unifying mental act. No-one would deny that some—not all—of Beethoven's late works demand much of the listener. But the difficulties, where they exist, do not lie where they have traditionally been said to lie—in the structure. They lie in the quality of the thought, and it need not surprise us that a great musical mind at the height of its powers is sometimes difficult to keep up with.

The C sharp minor fugue has the tonal outline:

C♯ minor (bars 1–31)
G♯ minor (bars 34–43)
modulatory process (bars 44–52)
B major-minor (bars 53–61)
A major (bars 63–72)
modulatory process (bars 73–82)
ornamented dominant suspense in C♯ minor (bars 83–92)
C♯ minor (bars 93–121)

That is to say, it fulfils the commonest expectations of a movement which begins by answering the tonic minor with the dominant minor. The relatively bright keys of B and A major provide the sensation of opposite tonal relation in the sense of minor-to-major (second to third main tonal area) following minor-to-minor (first to second main tonal area), in the manner described on page 81.

Ex. 15

BEETHOVEN: Quartet in C♯ minor, op. 131 - 1st movement

(a)

(b)

The tonal constitution of the B flat fugue of Op. 106 is shown on page 105:

The bar-numbers are included in the diagram because, although this is clearly a tonal structure, there may be difference of opinion as to how it should be interpreted.

The overall structure is a closed B flat, and is thus not open to question.

Two superimposed structures follow, the first D flat interlocking with G flat, and this one establishes the boundaries of the section. The second is an A flat structure, constituted internally as a mirror:

E♭ minor B♭ minor F minor A♭ F minor B♭ minor E♭ minor-major, the whole of this enclosed in A flat major.

What is significant to the overall structure of the work is that all these keys are on the dark side of B flat.

The complementary section which follows is essentially a D

major structure, with the first element of which a B minor structure interlocks. After this first element there is a middle section in G major, followed by the return of D in another symmetrical structure D—E♭—A♭—E♭—D.

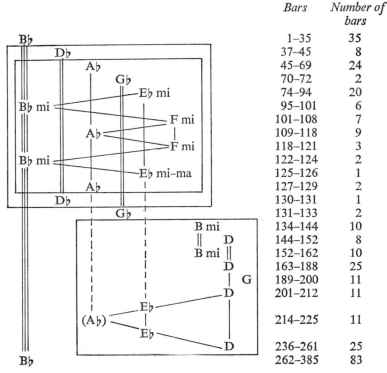

Bars	Number of bars
1–35	35
37–45	8
45–69	24
70–72	2
74–94	20
95–101	6
101–108	7
109–118	9
118–121	3
122–124	2
125–126	1
127–129	2
130–131	1
131–133	2
134–144	10
144–152	8
152–162	10
163–188	25
189–200	11
201–212	11
214–225	11
236–261	25
262–385	83

The relationship of D with the previous interlocking D flat/G flat might have been held to be ambiguous, but the process of arriving at it by way of B minor specifies its bright quality beyond a doubt. We thus have a home—dark—bright—home structure overall.

The A flat fugue in Op. 110 is very much simpler in tonal outline:

A♭ D♭ A♭ G minor | G major modulating to A♭

Thematically it is unusual, in that the G minor (dark-side) second main tonal area is provided by a restatement of the *arioso* which in A flat minor had acted as a prelude to the fugue. (Beethoven reaches it from the dominant-seventh chord of A flat by a characteristic 'sleight-of-hand' modulation which alters the seventh-chord by expansion to the second inversion of the tonic chord in G minor.)

The G major inversion of the fugal material which follows constitutes a section of opposite tonal relation after the dark-side G minor, and drifts off through C minor and E flat to the structural return of A flat.

Rondeau/Rondo

Baroque Rondeau

The group of structures expressing the principle of interspersed reiteration also repays study from the point of view of tonality, and four kinds of Baroque rondeau can—indeed, *must*—be distinguished.

I. The simplest defines its structure by the alternation of the theme (often self-repeating in its structure) with independent material of the same length as the theme, the total structure being completed by a final entry of the theme. Though there will almost certainly be tonal movement, the structure defined by it will be of a simple order: the first three structural elements in the tonic, perhaps, and the fourth—the second episode— either on the dark side or the bright, or even, in an undramatic fashion, successively both. Examples of this simplest kind of rondeau are however far outnumbered by more complex kinds.

II. The first of these is thematically, in terms both of the interleaving of episodes with the theme and of equality of length in its sections, precisely the same as the simplest kind discussed above. It differs in that it is tonally defined, the tonal relation between the first and second episodes opposing that between the first episode and the theme. When Lully uses this

Ex. 16

LULLY: 'Les Plaisirs de l' Ile enchantée' Rondeau pour les Flûtes et les Violons allant à la table du Roi

Ex. 17

PURCELL: 'Fear no danger to ensue' ('Dido and Aeneas')

structure he inclines to a 1—2—1—4—1 procedure, whereas Purcell's 'Fear no danger to ensue', in the first act of *Dido and Aeneas*, creates a 1—4—1—2—1 structure, (anticipating Beethoven's extension of classical resources by more than a century, but as it were casually, and with small-scale intentions).

III. The third kind, associated particularly with Couperin,

differs from the previous type only in the comparative length of its sections. But this difference is an important one since, combined with the defining use of tonality, it creates a structure framed in the same way as the large-scale thematically complex classical rondo. It differs from the second type of Baroque rondeau in its proportions, and from the first in its tonal construction. It too has an often self-repeating theme which appears at least three times, always in the tonic, finishing on the tonic chord. But its episodes need not be, and by definition not all of them can be, the same length as the theme. Episode 1 will move to a bright-side key (the dominant if the tonic is major, probably the relative major if the tonic is minor) and establish it. Episode 2 will be in opposite tonal relation: that is, on the dark side of the second tonality, the second having been on the bright side of the first. Thus the most promising aspect of the second type—its tonal definition—has been combined with an increase of flexibility in thematic proportions: a combination of importance for the rondeau's further development. For whenever tonal relations are established so as to take on more than primitive structural significance they assert control over consciously-apprehensible thematic factors; and the developed rondo of Haydn, Mozart and Beethoven is essentially, like this one though on a larger scale, a tonal structure (usually 1—2—1—4—1) of a relatively complex thematic character.

Couperin's *La Soeur Monique* exemplifies these characteristics, with the structure: $A_1 : B_2A_1C_4D_4A_1$ on A_1A_1. The procedure referred to as 'on A' consists of a variation on the first half of the rondeau theme repeated, followed by free material repeated. Thematically this is one of the factors that define the difference between this type of rondeau and its simpler predecessors—the factor of differing lengths of section. Tonally it is instructive in that, despite its free thematic form, the 'on A' procedure remains in the tonic key which returned with the previous statement of the rondeau theme.

The elements that constitute it are indicated in Ex. 18.

Ex. 18

COUPERIN: 'La Soeur Monique'

(a) Theme

(b) 1st couplet

(c) 2nd couplet

Couperin's *Les Moissonneurs* is a particularly revealing example of this type of structure, for at first sight or hearing it appears to complicate matters by having an extra *couplet* including an extra statement of the rondeau theme. (As we shall see, Rameau did write rondeaux with, in this sense, an 'extra' couplet and statement of the theme.) *Les Moissonneurs* proves to conform to the pattern of *Soeur Monique*, and its special manner of doing so is the cause of its special interest.

The theme is eight bars long, self-repeating and repeated. The first *couplet* is only four bars long (Ex. 19a), but in that short space moves to the dominant. The theme reappears, without repeat (Ex. 19b). The second *couplet* is eight bars long, referring thematically first to the first *couplet* and then to the theme (Ex. 19c). The theme follows, without repeat. The third *couplet* begins with a reference to the theme, starting in the tonic and moving to the supertonic minor. A similar reference leads to a firm cadence in C minor (Ex. 19d). What follows this turns out to be a process of ornamented dominant suspense leading to the final return of the rondeau theme. This third *couplet* is fourteen bars long.

The effect of this expanding series of *couplets* is that the first one, being so short, makes the group 'theme—*couplet*—theme', totalling sixteen bars of theme and four bars of *couplet*, sound like a unit whose middle section modulates to the bright side. Both the following couplets (separated by the third appearance of the theme) are on the dark side, the first in the relative minor of the tonic and the second in the relative minor of the subdominant. The necessity for the brief first *couplet* to move to the bright side, if the movement was to become a process of opposite tonal relation, is made clear, and it is hard to see how a composer could point more definitely to the principle underlying his structure. The warning should perhaps be added that there is here—of course—no intention to assert that musical structures *must* contain the process of opposite tonal relation. But we ought to be able to recognise it when it is there.

Ex. 19
COUPERIN; 'Les Moissonneurs'
(a) 1st half of theme (8 bars)

(b) *whole of 1st couplet (4 bars)*

(c) *half of 2nd couplet (8 bars)*

(d) *part of 3rd couplet (14 bars)*

IV. There is still a fourth kind of Baroque rondeau which, though it is historically less important, must be noted, if only to observe that it is different from the other three; for most traditional definitions of rondo proceed as if the thematic factor were the only interesting one, and the structure incapable of much refinement. We have seen that the simplest kind of rondeau (1) has equal lengths of thematic sections and is not tonally defined; that the second kind has equal lengths of thematic sections but *is* tonally defined; and that the third kind discussed in the previous paragraph has *un*equal lengths of thematic sections combined with tonal definition. The fourth kind, completing the mathematic possibilities of the set has neither equal lengths of thematic sections *nor* tonal definition. It is to be found in certain works of Rameau, and doubtless in those of other composers as well. Its procedures are that, rather than creating as do the other Baroque rondeaux the sensation of three or more appearances of a theme interspersed with other material, it reaches the ear as if it were starting out as an | : A : | | : BA : | structure but, instead of repeating its second element, replaces it with CA. So that the whole structure becomes | : A : | BA | CA (and sometimes DA as well). Why this sensation should exist, at any rate for some listeners, is hard to explain. It may be the combination of unequal thematic lengths (which are likely to be a good deal more unequal than in the case of type III), together with the lack of any essential tonal procedure, which makes each return of the rondeau theme seem more like a completion of the preceding episode than the recurrence of an independent entity. But since the phenomenon itself is not important, neither is it important to explain it: we may be content to note its existence.

Thus we have two kinds of Baroque rondeau (I and IV) in which tonality, though still basic in at least the sense of adherence to a tonal centre, is not strikingly important in the creation of contrasts; and two (II and III) in which the process of tonal opposition plays a vital part.

Classical Rondo

Since most classical concertos have a rondo for their last movement, it will be convenient here to conclude the discussion of that structure by reference to their procedures.

A rondo (or rondeau) of any type is normally defined as a structure in which one theme dominates all the others, partly by its character, which is gay and lively, and partly by its recurrence at least three times. Three times, that is to say, apart from repeats. Otherwise every two-part structure having two well-defined themes in its first part, and having its first part repeated, would tend to the character of rondo.

This definition, with one very slight modification, is satisfactory; and the modification is merely that in at least one movement of Mozart's—the last movement of the C major String Quintet, K. 515—everything is present to create an unmistakable sensation of his characteristic rondo, except that the theme, though continually hinted at and referred to, never makes its expected third appearance.

Two factors render this exception unimportant to the definition: first, that the failure of the theme to reappear can be held to be a humorous device; and second, that opponents of this first justification could assert that *since the theme does not reappear* (a qualification which implies that it was expected), the movement cannot be a rondo. This is tantamount to saying that it is a rondo in which the expected third statement of the theme is not allowed to reappear, and brings the second justification of the definition very close to the first.

The last movement of Mozart's fourth Violin Concerto, in D major, K. 218, is a characteristic example of what can become a structural torture-chamber for an intelligent student who supposes that what he reads in text-books about the structure of classical rondo must be true. He has been led to expect the rondo-theme, followed by material in a second key, the rondo-theme again (more or less complete), an episode (i.e., material of a well-defined thematic sort, which is neither the rondo-theme nor the material of the second main tonal area) or a 'development' (i.e., what would in the terminology of this book be called a section of opposite tonal relation expressed thematically by development of previously announced material), and the return of the rondo-theme on one side or the other, or both, of the material of the second main tonal area, now transposed to the tonic.

Up to the structural move to the dark side—the section of opposite tonal relation—which in this case takes the form of a developmental process on the last little tune of the rondo-theme modulating to the subdominant, all goes well. It is true that the first part of the rondo-theme is curiously fragmentary in character:

Ex. 20
MOZART: Violin Concerto in D, K.218 - last movement
(a)

extended to the dominant chord, repeated without the extension, and further extended by brief ornamentation of its last two notes. This is followed by:

(b)

(p)

extended by a coda-like procedure which, though it does not in fact constitute the end of the theme, is used repetitively to finish the movement:

(c)

(p)

The final fragment is also repeated, coming to the tonic instead of the mediant on its second appearance:

(d)

(p)   *fp*   *fp*

But a student who keeps his mind on the possibilities, as distinct from dogma, need not be unduly upset by that—until he begins to wonder whether the material which follows is still part of the theme, or part of a transition. For it drifts on in a series of little tunes, some of them repeated, until the listener cannot fail, if he is aware of the possibilities of such structures at all, to realise that the second main tonality has been established as it were behind his back.

The music slows to a halt on one of the fragments of the theme; the theme returns—nearly all of it, except that the final little tune, instead of repeating as it had done at first, moves off sequentially on the dark side.

So far, apart from some uncertainties, no major problems have arisen, and what follows conforms quite comfortably to the traditional definition. A clear-cut episode, consisting of two tunes—the second a 'musette'—appears in the appropriately dark-side key of the subdominant:

This is followed by material similar in character to that of this section's opening modulation to the dark side. (That was based on the last little tune of the theme, but this is entirely free material—in so far as any material can be quite unrelated which is based on such simple harmonic and melodic materials as the classicists customarily used.) This free material proceeds back to the tonic, in which, according to our student's expectation, either the material of the second main tonal area or the rondo-theme should now appear.

What does appear is a re-statement of the episode's first part (excluding the musette), given in the tonic and extended to a half-close, after which the third fragment *only* of the rondo-theme re-appears in the tonic, extended as at first and followed by a sizeable amount of the material of the second main tonal area, now in the tonic. After an extension leading to a cadenza —which usually signals the beginning of the coda—the third fragment (only) of the theme, extended in a slightly different fashion from before, re-appears and leads to the last, the antepenultimate and the penultimate little tunes of the theme, the first twice, the second twice and the third three times—and that's that. Now where is our conscientious student? He has had nothing like a complete re-appearance of the rondo-theme except in what he might reasonably regard as in the wrong place and the wrong order; and he has had—what he didn't expect and from the point of view of his preconceptions didn't want—a redundant entry of the dark-side episode, masquerading as the structural return by being in the home key. He is faced, in fact, by the two alternatives referred to earlier: either he lacks talent or his elders are wrong.

The second alternative, if his conscientiousness has reached disaster proportions, may never occur to him at all. But his elders are indeed wrong, if they have taught him the outlines of Classical rondo in any way which obscures the perfectly straightforward structural character of this movement.

The structural 'requirement' of a Classical developed rondo is no more than this: (1) The statement in the tonic of a theme which is more likely than not to be a clearly definable structure in its own right: an ABA or ABC structure or a two-part structure with perhaps (as in the last movement of Haydn's 102nd symphony) both its parts repeated. (2) Movement to and establishment of a second main tonality on the bright side of the first. In principle it could be the dark side, to be answered by the bright side, but I know no such example. Furthermore, nearly all Classical rondos are major as to their tonic, and since the invariable second main key after a major tonic, until Beethoven, is the dominant, this is the invariable key for this part of the structure in the rondos of Haydn and Mozart. (3) Return of the rondo-theme, either whole or in sufficient part to leave no doubt of its structural function, in the tonic. (4) Movement to the dark side, in which an episode may appear. (5) Return *to the tonic* (not to any particular thematic material), where the material of the second main tonal area will almost certainly be referred to and may return complete, and where the rondo-theme is very likely to return complete or may only be referred to.

The 'muddle', so to speak, of little tunes re-ordered from their appearance in the first part of the rondo under discussion is taken care of by the definition just given: that the return to the tonic is not accomplished by any particular thematic material. But what about the tonic appearance of the episode? If we base the structure on tonality, are we not saying—what is obviously not true—that the structural return occurs at the reappearance of the episode?

Not really. We shall see (p. 129) in setting out the procedures of the first movement of this concerto an example of a procedure frequent in the approach to the second main tonality. Namely, that where that tonality is to open, as a structural section, with a decisive tune, it is often approached by material which may spend quite a long time in the second main tonality itself. Similarly here, the *structural* return to the first key, which is expressed by material starting with the third fragment of the rondo-theme, is preceded by arrival in that key with material defining it as belonging structurally to the previous section. To express such a procedure in thematic material as decisive as that of the episode is unusual. But as long as we understand what is structurally afoot it is perfectly comprehensible as a whimsical ornament. No classical rondo *of this sort* will disturb our definition, though the differences of detail in such movements are innumerable. But there is another sort of classical rondo which does not conform to it, and therefore requires, not hatchet-work on the facts, but another definition.

This refers to a type of structure used by Mozart and Beethoven at least, in which the second appearance of the rondo-theme is not in the tonic, but in a key decisively on the dark side: a situation which defies the statement of even so good an analyst as R. O. Morris (in *The Structure of Music*), that 'it is a cardinal principle of rondo that every appearance of the rondo-theme must be in the tonic'. If the reader suspects that by dint of vast labours in dark corners of music we have dug up some exotic, egregious plant, let him be reassured—an example of what we shall call 'modulating rondo' (because the theme's change of key is essential to the structure) occurs as the last movement of Mozart's *Eine kleine Nachtmusik*. In this, the home key is G, the second main tonality D, in which the chief

Ex. 21

Mozart: Eine kleine Nachtmusik

(a)

p

(b)

tune is followed by an extended reference to the material of the first tune, still in the second tonality. The material up to that point is played twice, followed by a repetition of the link which led back to the beginning of the movement after the first statement of the two tonal areas.

(c)

At this point one has a slight sense of vertigo, for there seems momentarily no reason why the material so far announced should not go on circulating for ever. Rescue from this predicament comes in the form of an abrupt move to the key of E flat:

(d)

(Talk about Beethoven's sleight-of-hand modulations!)

The choice of this key for a new statement of the rondo theme is revealing. For the second statement—apart from repeats—of the theme itself constitutes, in a modulating rondo, the strongest sensation of the opposition of tonal relation in the movement. After it, in some cases, there is nothing more than a modulating process of structural return to the first key.

E flat, it will be noticed, is in the area of penumbra in relation to D, and cannot constitute a decisive dark-side relation to it. But by the time E flat appears D has already given way to the dominant-seventh chord of G, so that the sensation of darkness is related not to D but to G. Whether the process of tonal opposition, in the case of a rondo, is to relate to the immediately preceding tonic or to the second main tonal area is more theoretical than actual in application. For the tonic is on the dark side of its own dominant, so that any key which is on the dark side of the tonic is *a fortiori* on the dark side of the dominant.

After this, in the rondo of the Serenade, the structural return to the tonic is accomplished by normal processes of modulation, and the return itself is expressed by means of the material of the second main tonal area, transposed to the tonic, followed by the rondo theme in the tonic.

Mozart's Rondo for Piano, K. 485, follows the same procedures except that the key of the second statement of the rondo-theme (G major) is decisively on the dark side of the second main tonality (A major) as well as, inevitably, that of the tonic. The material following the structural return to the home key indulges in a series of tonal witticisms including the suggestion that the final statement of the theme is going to occur as far on the dark side of the tonic as you can get.

I conclude this account of classical rondo-structure with two oddities whose secrets I cannot unfold. The first may be called 'when is a rondo not a rondo?', and the second 'when is a two-part structure not a two-part structure?' Mozart wrote a 'Rondo alla Turca' as the last movement, in A minor, of the A major Piano Sonata. Its procedures are that first it states, by means of monothematic material, a characteristic two-part structure with both its parts repeated, moving from A minor to E minor in its first structural element.

Ex. 22

Mozart: Piano Sonata in A - last movement
(a)

It answers the ambiguity of the two minors relative to one another with the standard move to a major key—in this case C major—to produce the sensation of opposition of tonal relation.

(b)

The two-part structure ends with a return to the tonic minor by means of a version of the thematic material with which it began. So far an ordinary dance-movement structure. This is followed by a robust pseudo-'Turkish' tune in A major.

(c)

Then comes another two-part, monothematic structure, with both its parts repeated, in F sharp minor, moving to C sharp minor at the end of its first structural element and answering the two minors, as before, with the major key of A.

(d)

(e)

It returns to F sharp minor, with the same sort of thematic reference, for the conclusion of the two-part structure. This is followed by the pseudo-Turkish tune, again in A major. Then the first two-part structure is played again, in A minor, and a third statement of the pseudo-Turkish tune in A major leads to a thematically independent coda in the same key. This is like no rondo that ever was. (Wyzewa and Sainte-Foix, in volume 3 of their *Mozart*, refer to it as 'a typical example of French *rondeau*': a description which is generally held to refer to any of the kinds of Baroque rondeau which we have set out on pages 106–12. The reader is invited to solve the puzzle.)

What this rondo presents is a minuet-and-trio with a pseudo-Turkish tune between each of its parts, followed by a coda. It seems clear that Mozart—as often—was being funny: either by making his rondo-theme come in in the wrong place and be totally inadequate in any case to support the weight of the rest of the structure; or by implying that Turks characteristically do things backwards; or both. And the movement is a dreadful warning as to what will happen to analysts if they don't stay awake. For the greatest composers, like the greatest dramatists, cannot be depended upon to be unrelievedly sober-sided.

As to 'when is a two-part structure not a two-part structure?' there is in an unfinished keyboard suite by J. S. Bach, a movement entitled 'Sarabande en rondeau' which consists of a two-part structure, with both its parts repeated, thematically expressed as roughly | :A: | :BA: |. And that is all. It won't do to say 'Its editors, after all, entitled it "unfinished"—there was doubtless more to come', because there is no reason to suppose that *this movement* is unfinished—it is the suite that is so. Was it an invitation to add 'second sections', in the style of the Rameau rondeau to which we have referred, by means of improvisation? Unless we are to call every two-part structure with both its parts repeated, thematically expressed as | :A: | :BA: |, a rondeau (which would cover a very great deal of territory) there must be some such explanation, though I doubt whether this is the right one.

The Baroque Concerto

Corelli, Vivaldi and Handel clearly regard the medium of the concerto as in the main a means of producing agreeable music, imposing no severe demands on the listener. They all make much use of the processes of tonal opposition which we have discussed in the context of the fugue, and especially of the particular form of it expressed as *home—bright—dark—home*.

Thematically, Corelli deals in short alternations of theme fragments between *concertino* and *concerto grosso*; Handel in thematic outlines of larger scope, with few or none of the small-scale alternations characteristic of Corelli; Vivaldi in series of thematic fragments joined into continuous tunes, as Bach, and in another sense Mozart, would do, so that the fragments remain available for re-ordering on subsequent appearances. (One may venture the guess that it was perhaps this idiom of thematic fragments, to some extent held in common though differently handled, that led Bach to take the trouble of transcribing several of Vivaldi's concertos into other instrumentations.)

It is only with the concertos of Bach himself that we reach intertwined tonal and thematic characteristics of compelling analytical interest. The tonal aspect we have already disposed of, since it follows the same possibilities of procedure as those of his fugues: the home key at each end and a dark (or bright) section in the middle; the middle section, if dark, perhaps preceded and followed by sections bright in relation to the tonic, and perhaps, whether dark or bright, interrupted by material of opposite tonal relation to that of the section.

But thematically the concertos of Bach demand special attention because a number of his movements demonstrate a procedure particularly favoured by dramatic composers generally, from Monteverdi to Wagner. This procedure we shall, at an acceptable risk of confusion with medieval and Renaissance polyphonic structure of quite another kind, call a 'mirror-structure'. I have already used the term with reference to Bach's fugues (p. 95), where its application was sufficiently obvious that careful definition was hardly necessary. To define it specifically in a more complex situation the first movement of the first Brandenburg Concerto will serve, expressed by the symbols set out below, and referring to the tunes (Ex. 23):

Ex. 23

A_1 B_1 a_1 b_1 a^1_{seq} b^1_{seq} ext C_1

on A_{1-2} on $B_{II\ mi-rel\ mi-1}$ on C_4

on $B_{-rel\ mi}\ A_1$ a_1 b_1 a_1 b_1 ext $C_{rel\ mi}$ on $B_{mod}\ D_{1-2}$

A_1 a_1 b_1 a_1 b_1 ext $C_{2-III\ mi}$

on $B_{-II\ mi}\ a$ $b_{II\ mi}$ on B_{mod-1}

on A_{1-2} on $B_{-4}\ D_{4-1}$

A_1 B_1 a_1 b_1 a_1 b_1 ext C_1

A glance at the diagram taken as a mere series of symbols will satisfy the reader that the first line is answered by the last, the second by the sixth, the third by the fifth, and that the re-statement of most of the opening material in the dominant modulating to the mediant minor, forms a 'centre-piece' for the structure.

Taken by itself, this might be nothing more than a curiosity: an odd concatenation of circumstances in which the composer, thinking of the structure as tonally a '*home—(bright)—dark—dominant—dark—(bright)—home*' procedure (which it is) and thematically an ABA structure (which it is) had, perhaps half-consciously, perhaps entirely unconsciously, produced another ABA inside the first one and then another inside that.

But the first movement of the second Brandenburg is similar. Its structurally important tunes are seen in Ex. 24:

Ex. 24

BACH: Brandenburg Concerto No. 2 in F - 1st movement

and by reference to these the movement can be diagrammed as:

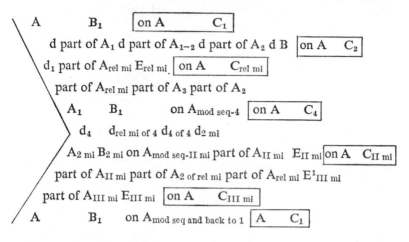

It may be objected that we had to ignore line 2 of the diagram to establish the mirror. As in all questions of consciously recognisable musical fact, the answer must be sought in the sound of music.

Musical 'symmetries', so-called, are not symmetries at all in the spatial sense of the term. In music, even the most important structural elements are required to balance each other exactly only in very sectional structures such as the minuet-and-trio. In more complex movements there is likely to be a process of reference—quite often on a large scale—to previously stated material rather than an unaltered re-statement of it.

Suppose in this movement we withdraw for a moment the question of the mirror and consider it only as an ABA structure. So much, in view of the decisive return to the opening material as finishing material, could scarcely be denied. Even so, the final 'A' is not identical with the first (though the final material in the first movement of the first Brandenburg is an exact replica of its opening). In the second concerto the final material of the movement, while fulfilling the structural function of reproducing the most important sensations created by the first, contains other material. The fact that we unhesitatingly accept this altered final section as structurally corresponding to the first is an acknowledgement of the nature of the so-called 'symmetries' in music, and justifies the assertion that the first structural element of this movement is a two-part procedure in which the function of the second part is to establish the dominant key without participating directly in the mirror-structure.

The material which follows returns as the penultimate element, the material which follows that returns as the antepenultimate element, and so on until the middle of the mirror is reached. But in this example the middle of the mirror is not represented by a re-statement of the opening material, as it had been in the first concerto, but by a sequential succession of appearances of the solo material whose omission at the end had raised our first doubts. It does have its day, after all—as the very centre-piece of the movement. It *could* recur yet again, just before the re-statement of the opening material, at the end of the movement, and so participate in the mirror in both places. But since music flows on in time—and therefore not only does not need, but for the most part positively rejects, the concept of spatial symmetry—it doesn't need to, and it doesn't.

The complexities of Bach's concerto structure do not exhaust themselves with the mirror character. They present two other aspects that need noting, the first thematic and the second the relation between all these thematic factors and tonality. In several cases of mirror-structure, and sometimes in cross-relation with it, there appears a reiterated section of music acting in several tonalities as a small finishing-piece to a series of 'running structures' (structures which constitute the temporal succession of the movement). Such a section is indicated in the diagram of the first movement of the first Brandenburg Concerto by the letter 'D' (bars 36–42), and it occurs just before the central appearance of the movement's main thematic group, and again just before the final appearance of that material. By appearing both times as the penultimate element of a structural section it crosses the mirror characteristic, which would require its second appearance to occur at the end of the fifth section, corresponding with the end of the third.

In the diagram of the first movement of the second Brandenburg Concerto, another such section is represented by the symbols 'on A C' (first appearing in bars 5–8), and it closes seven of the movement's ten sections. Here it is not in cross-relation with the mirror-structure, but emphasises it.

On the other hand, the mirror process and the *tonal* process generally coincide—in the Brandenburg examples always. If we represent the sections of the mirror by roman numerals, and tonality by our usual symbols, the structures—very much in outline—of the first movements of all the Brandenburgs except the fifth (which is not a mirror) will demonstrate the coincidence of the two processes:

1. I_1 ref to I_2 II III_4 I_2 III II_4 ref to $I_2 I_1$
2. $I_1 II$ with part of $I_{1-2} III_4$ ref to $I_{4-2} I^1_{1-4} II_4 I^2_4$ ref to $I_4 III_4 I_1$
3. I ext $_{1-2-4-1}I_1 II_4$ fugal expo on $I_1 II^1_4$ I ext (short) I^2_i
4. I_1 II_{1-4} III_4 II_{4-1} III_{1-4} I_1
6. I_1 ext $_{1-2-1}$: II_{1-2-4}: part of II_4 II reversed $_{4-2-1}$ I^1_1

It would be no more than proper for the reader to be sceptical about the reality of such mirror structures. Partly because their existence, if it is real, has escaped the attention of analysts for so long; and partly because, at first sight, there is something improbable to the musician in the idea of musical structures proceeding so as to contravene the coincidence of temporal and structural succession. A prejudice against such an idea is understandable, but it will not bear examination. If it were strictly justifiable, music would not be able at any time to refer to its previous events, whereas in fact such reference is of the very essence of musical structure. Regarded in this way, it becomes clear that, if we can form a structure by letting the opening material re-appear after intervening material, and if we can extend such a procedure further by following the second appearance of the opening material with still more new material and a final re-appearance of the first, then it is equally possible, though perhaps more whimsical, to allow the second part of a movement to present in reverse order the series of events which had constituted its first part. As we have seen, in the nature of musical 'symmetry', these events are not likely to be either uninterrupted or precisely the same as they were before.

The Classical Concerto

Haydn and Mozart

The classical concerto characteristically uses for its first move-ment the same structure as that of the symphony (or a similar work-in-several-movements for any medium). It precedes it with what we shall call—the phrase being expressionless and without misleading associations—an 'orchestral statement of themes'. It is this, as Tovey pointed out, which enables the concerto as Mozart designed it to have the subtle inter-relations of internal structure that it has, and the elusive difference between the Classical and the Romantic attitude towards the function of structure can hardly be more clearly seen than in the Romantic rejection of the orchestral statement of themes in the concerto and Brahms' re-establishment of it.

Haydn preferred, as did Johann Stamitz the elder, to have a structural change of key in the course of this orchestral state-ment, and Beethoven followed suit in his first three published concertos.

A structural key-change in the orchestral statement of themes, if it leads to the same key as is to be used for the second main tonality in the sonata-form element, has the disadvantage of anticipating that tonality. This is no fatal flaw, or Haydn and Beethoven would never have used it. But it has neither the advantages of the complete duplication of a sectional repeat nor those of the tonal stability of Mozart's procedure, and Beethoven, having driven it to its logical conclusion by produc-ing the one and only double exposition among classical con-certos of importance, adopted thereafter Mozart's method.

Tovey and Hutchings between them have said everything of major importance about Mozart's concerto structure, and it will suffice here to set out the procedures of the D major Violin Concerto, K. 218, in relation to the present hypothesis.

As its 'statement of themes' for the first movement, the orchestra sets out the following tunes:

Ex. 25
MOZART: Violin Concerto in D, K.218 1st movement

This material is brought to a cadence before the appearance of:

which is followed by extensive material based on:

and four small, repetitive tunes of a coda-like sort.

Thus, as a means of clarifying the relation between the orchestral statement of themes and the sonata exposition which follows, we can state the former as:

$$a\ b\ c\ c\ \text{ext}\ d\ d^1\ e\ f\ g\ g\ h\ i$$

all of it being in the tonic.

The material of the first main tonal area of the sonata exposition starts with tunes *a* and *b*, but follows them with a new piece of material brought to a cadence with the last of the

TMS—I

tunes of the orchestral statement. There is then an extensive area of new material of a formula sort, which modulates quite early to the dominant and stays there. But it is not yet the material which is to define structurally the second main tonality of the movement. This begins with the tune *d*, and the second main tonal area consists largely of the material which had followed that tune in the orchestral statement. Thus the first and second main tonal areas can be diagrammed as:

$$a\ b\ ji_1 K_{1-2} L_2\ M_2\ N_2\ d_2\ d_{2\text{mi}}\ e^1{}_{2\text{ma}}\ \textit{ext to cadence}\ gg_2\ hh_2$$

The section of opposite tonal relation starts briefly with a brief reference to the tune *K* which is extended by means of similar, but actually free material. It modulates through the relative minor, the supertonic minor, the dominant, the tonic, the subdominant; thence back through the supertonic minor again to the dominant chord of the tonic.

The structural return to the home key is defined, *not*, as we have been 'conditioned' to suppose, by the first material of the first main tonal area, but by the material which started moving to the *second* main tonal area: the material referred to above as *K*. Most of the material which initially followed *K* returns, with the insertion of the tune *c* immediately after *K* and the tune *f*, which had been omitted from the second main tonal area, before the return of *d*. The tune *c* appears again just before the extension of the tonic cadence to the $\frac{6}{4}$ chord which precedes the cadenza, and the movement finishes with the material which had finished the orchestral statement of themes.

The device of leaving the tune *c* unheard after its first appearance until after the section of opposite tonal relation is, though common with Mozart, not peculiar to him. Bach used it also, as for example in the first movement of the first Brandenburg Concerto, where the material extending from bar 3 to bar 5 does not re-appear until the exact restatement of the whole first material at the end of the movement.

The emphasis on the tune *d* as the beginning of a new section in the orchestral statement of themes, that tune being the one which is to begin the material of the second main tonal area in the sonata exposition that follows, is characteristic of Mozart's concerto procedure.

The extensive material in the second main tonality starting in the course of *K* could indeed be regarded as a Haydnesque example of the composer allowing the material to 'drift' into the second main tonality so that that tonality is recognised in Haydn's fashion some time after the event, as having been established *de facto*. But Mozart is making the best of both worlds by emphasising the appearance of *d* in such a way that it gives the impression of starting the second main tonal area, even though its tonality is the same as that of the preceding material.

The section of opposite tonal relation, though it refers to *K* at its start, is not a development. Its 'oppositeness' of tonal relation is not undermined by the appearances of the dominant and the tonic, which occur in the course of a modulatory process constituting the whole section and bounded by minor keys.

The slow movement of this concerto, besides being musically exquisite, provides a microcosm of almost everything that Mozart regards as important in his first-movement concerto structure. It lacks only a section of opposite tonal relation, which is replaced by a process of dominant suspense which leads to gravely humorous consequences when it returns, inevitably as dominant suspense in the subdominant, following the reiteration of the opening material in the tonic throughout.

Apart from this, it has an orchestral statement of themes, one of whose themes remains unheard until after the suspense process which takes the place of a section of opposite tonal relation; the last tune of the orchestral statement is so designed that it can lead either to the tonic, by being played complete, or to the dominant by staying there after it gets there; it reintroduces the 'unheard' tune after the cadenza, following it with the tune which followed it in the orchestral statement of themes; and, after two references to the opening tune of the movement, altered to a coda-like character, it closes demurely with the second tune of the movement which had always led either to the third or to an extension of itself, and which until it happens sounds as if it could not possibly finish anything.

Its materials are:

Ex. 26

MOZART: Violin Concerto in D, K.218 - 2nd movement

and its diagram can be set out as:

Orchestral statement of themes	a b c_1 d_{1-2-1}
First and second main tonal areas	a b ext to cadence$_1$$d_{1-2}$ ext$_2$e e f g $g^1{}_2$h dom suspense in 1
Structural return to home key	a b ext to cadence$_1$$d_{1-2-1}$e e f g $g^1{}_1$h dom susp in 4 ext −1
Coda	Cadenza cd_{1-2-1} on a twice$_1$$b_1$

Beethoven

With Beethoven, it is worth setting out the clearest 'auto-biography' of a composer's developing thought in a given area of composition that our tradition affords. Of the three great classicists, as we see them approaching the concerto problem, Haydn seemed to give it no special attention, Mozart did it, as with everything, apparently by magic, and Beethoven is the one whom we can see—not in books, but in the music—engaged in mortal struggle with a structural problem.

Though the first concerto to be published was written in 1795, revised in 1797-8, published after the C major concerto, and known as No. 2, from the point of view of our interest in its place in Beethoven's concerto-autobiography it is clearly No. 1. The tonal procedures of its first two structural elements—the orchestral statement of themes and the sonata-form exposition—which are followed to the letter by those of the second concerto—are these.

The tonic is established by means of material beginning:

Ex. 27

BEETHOVEN: Piano Concerto No. 2 in Bb - 1st movement

and ending with this procedure to the dominant chord of the dominant key:

By a typical sleight-of-hand modulation Beethoven moves to the remote key of D flat expressed in a new tune:

and returns to the tonic major, by way of its own minor—the relative minor of D flat—for the conclusion of the orchestral statement of themes.

The first structural element of the movement in sonata-form begins with a third new tune:

followed by references to the opening material of the orchestral statement of themes, which lead to the expected dominant for still a fourth new tune:

Particularly in view of the appearance of the same procedure in the C major piano concerto, it is notable that immediately after this fourth tune had been repeated by the solo piano, the music subsides into D flat again for still another tune—but this time not a structurally important one.

Each of the main tonalities—B flat and D flat in the orchestral statement of themes; B flat and F in the sonata exposition—is expressed by means of a different tune, and from the point of view of the 'autobiography' the point of interest is that there is here *maximum difference*, both thematically and, except that both the orchestral statement and the sonata exposition start in the tonic, tonally. There is no solo rhapsody between the two elements, and, though the first tune of the sonata exposition is, as has been noted, a new one, it is followed by reference to the first tune of the orchestral statement of themes.

The C major concerto, written in 1797, follows precisely the same tonal pattern as that of the B flat, but it expresses the second main tonal area in the sonata exposition by means of the same tune which had appeared in the abruptly reached dark-side key of E flat in the orchestral statement.

Ex. 28

BEETHOVEN: Piano Concerto No. 1 in C major - 1st movement

Thus we see the composer drawing back a little from the concept of *maximum* difference: there is now maximum difference less one theme.

Simply as a logical possibility we can project a hypothetical structure for these areas of the first movement in a third concerto if Beethoven were to write one. For if you start from a position of maximum difference and move in the direction of reducing that difference, one of the possibilities for the next move is clearly to jump to the other end of that scale and express maximum sameness. That Beethoven does this is remarkable; but what is even more remarkable is the degree of sameness in detail with which he chooses to do it. Having established the first tonal area of the orchestral statement of themes he moves to the relative major as the second tonal area. He does this by means of a process of dominant suspense in the minor mode of the new key, thereafter returning inevitably to the tonic for the completion of the orchestral statement. The procedures, both tonal and thematic, of the first two main tonal areas of the following sonata exposition are in a structural sense, precisely the same except for their exclusion of the return to the tonic. They include the same opening tune (without intervening rhapsody) in the tonic minor, the same process of dominant suspense in the minor mode of the relative major, the same tunes in the relative major for the second main tonal area.

So far Beethoven has been following the tradition of Stamitz and Haydn: the assumption that the orchestral statement of themes, if it is of considerable size, should have a structural key-change and a return to the tonic within it. The keys he chooses to use move much further afield than Haydn's, as his general broadening of conception in tonal relations would lead us to suppose likely. But they fulfil the same structural function as Haydn's dominant. In the first two concertos he creates between the orchestral statements of themes and their sonata expositions the same situation of opposite tonal relation as Brahms does in the double concerto: the second key of the orchestral statement being on the dark side of that of the exposition (Beethoven, B flat concerto: B♭—D♭ B♭—F; C major concerto: C—E♭ C—G; Brahms, double concerto: A minor—F A minor—C). But having moved from maximum difference to maximum sameness, Beethoven seems to make up his mind that Mozart was right after all: that a concerto structure characterised by a preliminary orchestral statement of themes can reach a higher stage of refinement if that statement of themes holds altogether aloof from the tonal procedures which will come into play in the sonata exposition.

The Triple Concerto of 1804–5 institutes an era lasting to the surprisingly early end of Beethoven's concern with the concerto problem. An era in which by various means as to detail he uses Mozart's system of relationship between the orchestral statement of themes and the sonata exposition. The Triple Concerto is as clear an example of it as is the E flat Piano Concerto—the last of the seven—and it is noteworthy that Beethoven does not arrive at this change of mind through a struggle as to *what* to do if he abandons Haydn's method of tonal relationship: when he changes he does so abruptly and conclusively, suggesting that there were in his mind only the two alternatives. Having tried out the first from maximum difference to maximum sameness he moves to the other alternative with complete confidence and clarity. (Is it extravagant to suppose that the exposition's far-flung A major-to-minor-to-major for the second main tonal area may derive from the composer's propensity for wide-ranging tonal procedures and the fact that he had just denied himself one possibility?)

The drama of the voyage is now over, for Beethoven is safe home in a port which he never, apparently, had any inclination to leave.

The wider-ranging ornamental modulations of the G major concerto belong perhaps with the adventurous quality of some of the piano sonatas as evidence of the 'at-home' feeling that even so great a composer as Beethoven may have had in writing for the instrument on which his own virtuoso powers as performer were displayed. For of the four concertos written after his conversion to Mozart's way of thinking, only the Fourth Piano Concerto ranges so freely in ornamental modulation in its orchestral statement of themes. Yet the repetitive cast of a composer's mind—any artist's mind—shows here in that, just as he is breaking away from the tonal pattern of his earlier concertos, he reverts to an aspect of the thematic difference which had characterised those earlier works. In the first concerto he had expressed the second main tonality of the sonata exposition by means of a tune which had not appeared in the corresponding position—or indeed anywhere—in the orchestral statement of themes. This aspect of difference has not appeared since: neither in the second nor in the third. But now he introduces a version of it by beginning the second main tonal area of the fourth concerto with a new and very decisive tune: one so 'catchy' in character that, knowing the work as well as we are bound to do if we listen to music at all, it comes as a surprise to realise that it has not been heard until this moment of the structure.

Ex. 29

BEETHOVEN: Piano Concerto No. 4 in G - 1st movement

The Violin Concerto, written in 1806, is as straight-forwardly Mozartian in structure—though naturally as Beethovenian in content—as the Triple Concerto. Its main unexpectedness comes in its almost casual repetition of the whole of the material constituting the second main tonal area. It arrives at that repetition by another tonal joke. The only considerable obscuring of the first key which occurs in the orchestral statement of themes takes the form of an abrupt move to the *chord* of B flat, which never has time to become the *key* of B flat because the music very shortly moves back chromatically to the dominant chord of the tonic D, whereupon the material which will later form that of the second main tonal area of the exposition has its first hearing.

Ex. 30

BEETHOVEN: Violin Concerto in D - 1st movement

The exposition moves from the first to the second main tonal area without mentioning this abrupt dark-side material, but reintroduces it after the completion of the material of that area. In the orchestral statement of themes the dark-side plunge had led to a statement of this same material and now it does so again, but related to the dominant instead of the tonic.

Thus in the sonata exposition of this work the second element is repeated and the first is not: a state of affairs which throws light on the attitude of structural-minded composers towards the matter of repeats. It used to be said by people who ought to have known better—and they supported their words by deeds in performance—that repeat marks had been used by composers of the Baroque and Classical periods because the audiences of those old days were unsophisticated and would be unable to hold the thematic material in their heads long enough to recognise it in development unless it was played twice. Nobody ever mentioned why the second half of the structure, on this hypothesis, should have been repeated at all. What's more, nobody ever mentioned why such two-part structures as the last movement of the F minor Piano Sonata (the *Appassionata*), the theme of the slow movement in the Seventh Symphony and that of the 'Ode to Joy' in the Ninth Symphony, should repeat their second section without repeating their first. Composers repeat sections of their music when they want music of sectional character to increase its size without increasing its complexity. To leave out a repeat is therefore to accuse the composer of failure in design—as becomes apparent when conductors fail to repeat the parts of the scherzo in the Ninth Symphony. When the scherzo and its trio have been played and the scherzo has returned once, Beethoven feints in the direction of his elsewhere-used procedure of starting the trio over again, with the implication that the scherzo will also return, for the third time. The scherzo, played with its repeats, is of such magnitude that the listener is conscious of a certain feeling of protest at the possibility of so large an extension of the sectional material; and Beethoven's abrupt 'Stand-down!' is precisely in its place. But when the repeats of the scherzo are left out one could perfectly well hear the trio and scherzo once again; so the wrench to a stop, seeming needless, fails in its purpose.

After the Violin Concerto there is concerto-silence for nine years. Are we straining the argument in suggesting that, the problem being solved, there was no urgency? In any case the E flat Piano Concerto when it comes, hugely monumental as it is, presents no aspects of the concerto-problem that Beethoven has not addressed himself to and solved before. The orchestral statement of themes is firmly in the tonic throughout, the material which is to become that of the second main tonal area —or rather, that of its beginning—being in the tonic minor.

There are, however, a number of events of an ornamental sort which emphasise the importance of simplicity in structural outline so that the mind of the composer can play freely in the subtlety of its presentation. The most obvious of these is the choice of B *natural* minor as the first key of the second main tonal area; a key which alters abruptly to the expected B *flat* major for that part of the thematic material which had appeared in the orchestral statement of themes in the tonic major after the tonic minor. The procedure, quite undisturbing to the basic pattern of the movement, manifests again Beethoven's preference for extending ornamentally the tonal areas which he keeps so clear-cut structurally, and also his enjoyment of the sensation of surprise introduced by the presentation of structurally important material in what is apparently the 'wrong' key. We have already noted this tendency with regard to the 'framing' of sections of opposite tonal relation in bright-side material. More interesting in the E flat concerto however is the extreme symmetry of the thematic material from the beginning of the introduction to the end of the coda.

Of the three great classicists, Beethoven was the one most given to thematic symmetries: a fact which has led analysts to make extravagant statements about the degree of thematic symmetry normally to be expected in classical structures. In the large-scale rondo, for example, Beethoven's preference was for the return to the first tonality, after the section of opposite tonal relation, to restate first the rondo-theme, then the material of the second main tonal area (transposed to the tonic), then the rondo-theme again. This, as has often been pointed out, taken together with the two appearances of the rondo-theme, separated by the material of the second main tonal area, which have appeared *before* the section of opposite tonal relation, creates a structure strongly marked by thematic symmetry. But it is not at all characteristic of the developed rondos of Haydn and Mozart, who are more inclined to one or other of the other two thematic possibilities for the structural return to the tonic: either the rondo-theme followed by the material of the second main tonal area, with *no* further return of the rondo-theme, or the rondo-theme *following* the material of the second main tonal area.

The thematic symmetry of the first movement of the E flat concerto is so marked as to create an overall mirror-structure consisting of A A^1 B A^{1}A, in which B is itself a mirror-structure. Expanding the diagram somewhat, the procedures of the movement can be expressed as:

OST	Introduction V_1 W_1 mi–ma X_1	$=$A
1st & 2nd main		
tonal areas	V_1 W''_2'' mi–ma XZ_2	$=$A^1
SOTR [on V] end of X formula I Z		
formula II end of X		$=$XZX$=$B
Return to		
1st key	Introduction V_1^1 W_1 mi–ma X_1	$=$A^1
Coda	Cadenza W_1 mi–ma end of X_1	$=$A

The coda contains no thematic material represented in the diagram as V, and it presents only the end of X instead of the whole of it; but since as a 'running structure' its primary function is to act as a finishing piece one would not expect it to exhibit the degree of complete statement which characterises the preceding areas. Nevertheless, a sceptical reader may feel that these omissions render the representation of the coda as A rather than A² a piece of special pleading in favour of the suggested mirror-structure diagnosis. But if the suggestion is withdrawn, to be replaced by the diagram A A¹ B A¹ coda we have still to recognise that the coda is of a thematic character so closely conforming to the outlines of the previous sections as inevitably to force the recognition of a certain mirror-like character in the whole. And since musical mirrors of this (as distinct from the medieval-contrapuntal) sort are never literally exact, the two statements are scarcely distinguishable in their implications. (A similarly characteristic inexactitude is introduced by the appearance of material based on V at the beginning of the section of opposite tonal relation. It is outside the symmetrical scheme, acting as an introductory procedure before the main material of the section gets under way (and in this it is characteristic of a good many classical works of the sort); but

Ex. 31

BEETHOVEN: Piano Concerto No. 5 in E♭ - 1st movement

(a) Introduction

BEETHOVEN CONCERTOS—ORCHESTRAL STATEMENTS AND SONATA EXPOSITIONS

Concerto	Key	Date	Opus No.	Orchestral Statement of Themes	Solo Fantasia	Sonata Exposition
Piano 2	B♭	1795-8	19	$A_{B\flat}$ - - - - - $B_{D\flat}$-B♭ mi-ma	—	$C_{B\flat}$ refs to A - - - - - -D_F
Piano 1	C	1797	15	A_C - - - - - $B_{E\flat}$-C mi-ma	—	C_C refs to A - - - - -B_G
Piano 3	C mi	1800	37	A_{Cmi} [E♭ ma–mi / dom susp] - - $B_{E\flat}$-Cmi	Very brief rising scales	A_{Cmi} - [E♭ ma–mi / dom susp] - - - $B_{E\flat}$
Triple	C	1804-5	56	A_C - - - - -B_C	—	A_C - - - - -$B_{A\ ma\text{-}mi\text{-}ma}$
Piano 4	G	1805-6	58	Intro$_{(on\ A)}$ $A_G B$ with refs to $A_{mod} C_G D_G A^1_G$	Extensive	On intro A^2_G -$E_\flat B_{mod} C_D D_D A^1_D$
Violin	D	1806	61	A_D - - - - -$B_{D\ ma\text{-}mi\text{-}ma}$	Extensive	A_D - - - - -$B_{A\ ma\text{-}mi\text{-}ma}$
Piano 5	E♭	1815	73	Intro$_{(I\text{-}IV\text{-}V^7)}$ $A_{E\flat}$ - - - $B_{E\flat mi\text{-}ma}$ on $A_{E\flat}$	Rising chromatic scale under orchestral dom chord	On A to on end of $A_{E\flat}$ $B_{Bmi\text{-}B\flat ma\ (-G)}$

its presence does nothing to undermine the well-defined structure of the section proper).

The materials referred to are shown on page 142.

INTERLOCKING VARIATION-FORM

Beethoven's special sort of variation-form is an expression of his preference for wider scope than his predecessors had used in the structural as well as the ornamental relationships of keys.

There are at least four examples of this special form: the slow movements of the Fifth, Seventh and Ninth symphonies, and that of the A minor String Quartet, Op. 132. Three of these submit to expression through one generalisation and will be dealt with together. The slow movement of the Seventh Symphony, though clearly expressing the same basic principle of structure as the others, shows enough difference of detail that it will be convenient to treat it separately.

This structure consists of a theme and at least one variation of that theme, interlocking with another theme, which it will be convenient to call an episode, tonally far on the bright side of the first, and at least one variant of that episode. (The word 'variant' is used here to refer to alteration of the theme limited to ornamentation, resulting in changes a good deal less developed than those of a variation.) Further appearances of the episode will be either in the same very-bright key (in relation to the first) in which it first appeared, or in another key, also far on the bright side of the first. The number of variations on the main theme varies in the examples to be discussed between one (in the string quartet) and five (in the Fifth Symphony). The number of variants on the episode varies between one (in all but the Fifth) and two (in the Fifth). There is always an extensive coda, even when it consists—as in the Seventh Symphony—largely of a variation on the main theme. The codas in the other three works do not contain a complete variation on the main theme but make extensive reference to it.

The simplest example of this structure occurs in the A minor String Quartet, Op. 132. (Ex. 32a and b.)

Ex. 32

(a) Main theme

Variation on main theme   Lydian mode on F
Variant of episode   D major
Coda (on main theme)   Lydian mode on F

The key-scheme immediately shows—what is true of all the examples—that the structure has the character of a tonal rondo.

On the thematic side, the variant of the episode in this instance is sufficiently different from what the episode was at its first appearance to justify the objection that the distinction between a variation and a variant is becoming blurred. Indeed, this movement taken alone would not have given rise to the definition. It is the likeness of the movement in all other respects to the basic procedures of the three symphonic examples which brings it into the same category with them.

TMS—K

The materials of the slow movement in the Fifth Symphony are shown in Ex. 33.

Ex. 33
BEETHOVEN: Symphony No. 5 in C minor - 2nd movement

(a) Main theme

Reiteration of final notes of Extension 2

Repetition of reiteration, with reiteration of tonic

A great tune? Undoubtedly. And an instructive lesson in the improbable materials from which a great tune can be built.

The episode, in the very bright key—relative to A flat—of C major, is equally improbable, consisting of nothing but tonic and dominant chords:

(b)

sempre ff

sf

With these as its main materials the movement is built as follows:

Main theme, with extensions	A flat major
Transition, starting with an anticipation of the material of the episode; A flat modulating to	
Episode	C major
Extension of episode material effecting transition to	
Variation 1 on main theme, with extensions	A flat
Transition as before, modulating to	
Variant 1 of Episode	C major
Extension as before, modulating to	
Variation 2 on main theme, without extensions	A flat
Variation 3 on main theme, without extensions	A flat
Variation 4 on main theme, without extensions	A flat
Dominant suspense in the dominant key, leading to	

Variant 2 of Episode, without extension	C major
Dominant suspense in the tonic, leading to	
material based on the main theme, in the	A flat minor
tonic minor (far on the dark side) leading to	
Variation 5 on main theme, with extensions	A flat
Coda, based on the main theme, starting on	
the dark side and modulating home	

Tovey called this movement 'unique', but, in relation to the three other examples here described, its uniqueness lies only in ornamental factors: its use of transitions, its set of three successive variations on the main theme shorn of its extensions, and its second variant on the episode.

After a brief, dominant-suspense introduction, the main materials of the slow movement in the Ninth Symphony are:

Ex. 34
BEETHOVEN: Symphony No. 9 in D minor - 2nd movement
(a) Main theme

mezza voce

(b) Episode

espressivo

p cresc.

On these, the movement is built as follows:

Introduction	dominant suspense in B flat
Main theme	B flat
Episode	D major
Variation 1 on theme	B flat
Variant of Episode	G major
Development of material of theme on	Section of opposite
dark side, modulating E flat to C flat	tonal relation
Variation 2 on theme	B flat
Coda, starting with fanfare in E flat and	
using considerable stretches of the	
theme in B flat where it inevitably	
concludes.	B flat

This movement gives us ample justification for using the word 'effrontery' with regard to Beethoven's modulations. For the move from B flat to D is made by the outrageous process of moving to what in the context can only be the dominant chord of the relative (G) minor and blandly using it as if its mere presence had fully established the key of D. One cannot deny that, in retrospect, it has. When the same procedure comes round again at the end of the first variation of the theme, the same chord of D major in its first inversion is used as the dominant chord of G (i.e., the major mode of the relative minor), establishing it in a manner only just less bare-faced than the first. To cap it all the return to B flat after the dark-side area is effected by chromatic alteration of three notes of the dominant chord of C flat to form the second inversion of the tonic chord of the home key: F flat to F natural, D flat to D natural, and, by implication, G flat to F, while the B flat remains as common to them both.

A composite diagram will show the relation of each of the four movements to the basic procedures of the structure (see p. 150).

The basic procedures are seen to be, as they were at first described: (i) the appearance of a main theme and one or more series of variations, all in the home key; (ii) the appearance of an episode and not more than two variants, both (or all) in a tonality far on the bright side of the home key. The Ninth Symphony is the only example which puts the second appearance of the episode in a key other than that of its first appearance. (iii) The interlocking of these procedures.

The diagram also makes clear why it was desirable to postpone the discussion of the Seventh Symphony's example until the others had been made clear. Though it is unmistakably of the same basic sort, it complicates description as a generalisation by placing the first appearance of its episode *after* the first set of variations on the main theme; by keeping its development process (a fugato) in the tonic; by making the following variation on the main theme a mere reference to its first and last

Event	Main theme	Episode	Var(s) on Th.	Ep. or Vnt 1 on Ep.	Var(s) on Th.	Dom susp.	Vnt 2 on Ep.	Dom susp.	Dev	Var on Th.	Vnt 1 on Ep.	Coda
Tonality	Home	Very bright	Home	Very bright	Home	(1)	Very bright	(2)	Dark or home	Home	Very bright	Home
5th												
7th												
9th												
132												

Transitions
(Fifth Symphony only)

bars and much abbreviating the following variant on the
episode; and by placing a complete variation on the main
theme within the coda. The tonal scheme of the fugato stems
from the fact that the minor tonic is answered by the minor
dominant twice—creating the sensation, in the following context, of a repeated first part of a two-part structure. The process
of opposite tonal relation normal to the tonic-minor-dominant-
minor situation then occurs, by means of the relative major of
the tonic as a bright key (minor-to-major after minor-to-minor).
This is followed by another major key—therefore still bright in

Ex. 35

BEETHOVEN: Symphony No. 7 in A - 2nd movement

(a) *Main theme*

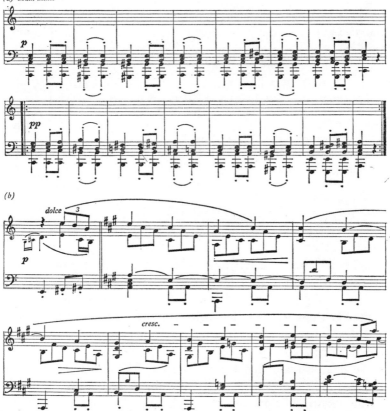

(b)

relation to the first element of the structure—which, since it is the subdominant of the relative major, creates a move to the dark side of that key and thus a double process of tonal opposition. The fugato finishes, as has already been mentioned, in the tonic minor.

Its main materials are shown in Ex. 35a and b on the previous page and its procedures in diagrammatic form are shown below:

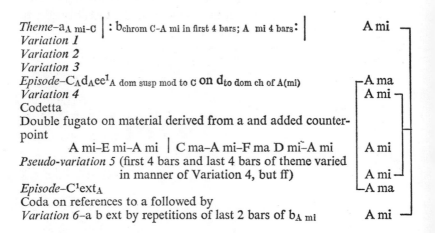

BEETHOVEN'S LAST QUARTETS

Beethoven's last quartets have often been used as evidence that in his third period he left Classical structure behind and used unheard-of procedures. It is true that there has been nothing quite like these works either before or since, but in them nothing untoward happened to the essential procedures of Classical sonata-form.

To demonstrate this I shall use Op. 127 and 130, analysing most of their movements tonally, from the beginning to the end of the section of opposite tonal relation.

Quartet in E flat major, Op. 127

FIRST MOVEMENT
Home key: E flat, expressed as:

Ex. 36

(a) BEETHOVEN: String Quartet No. 12 in E♭, op. 127 - 1st movement

Second main tonality, on the dark side of home, expressed as:

Section of opposite tonal relation

G major bright side of second main tonality¯expressed as:

A modulatory process through C minor, A flat, B flat minor, to the chord of C major as the dominant of F minor. C major (continuing the dark side of G major which was begun by the modulating process, but also acting as the bright side of G minor), expressed as:

After a brief formula process of F minor—A flat—F minor, the structural return to the first tonality is achieved by means of the first main tune of the Allegro at bar 167. The material of the second main tonality reappears to create a sensation of thematic symmetry, transferred from G minor to the tonic major.

This movement, so troublesome if Classical structure is analysed primarily in terms of themes, conforms with special subtlety to the definition 'home—second main tonality—process of opposite tonal relation—home'.

Since the second key is on the dark side of the first, the section of opposite tonal relation will involve keys on the bright side of the second; and in this case Beethoven has chosen to put them on the bright side of the first as well.

The subtlety arises from the use of G major as the first tonal element of the section. This key has in the context a dual character. As a change of mode on the same tonal centre as that of the second main key section it demonstrates the frequent classical procedure of beginning the section of opposite relation with a continuation of the second main key. But *because* it changes the mode it acts already as an 'opposite', and furthermore enables the next appearance of the *Maestoso* material, in C major, to have also a dual character. Its primary function is fulfilled as a key on the bright side of the second main tonality. But it is also on the dark side of that part of the section of opposite relation which was itself (in one of its aspects) a continuation, altered in mode, of the second main tonality. Because most second main keys in the Classical period are on the bright side of the tonic, the section of opposite tonal relation is chiefly associated with a descent to the dark side; the procedure here thus makes a cross-reference to the listener's commonest experience of such contexts.

Alternatively it can be taken that the G major appearance of the opening tune represents Beethoven's not infrequent procedure of using a double-tonality unit, minor to major in character, as his second main tonal area—in this case G minor-to-major—in which case the C major appearance is the normal process of opposite tonal relation to G. We shall have further occasion to note such procedures in discussing the means by which Brahms adapted Classical structure to his needs.

SECOND MOVEMENT—SCHERZO
Home key: E flat, expressed in Ex. 37.

Ex. 37

BEETHOVEN: String Quartet No. 12 in E♭, op. 127 - 2nd movement

This moves through a $4 + 3 + 2$ rhythmic procedure to a second main tonality (the dominant) little more than a quarter of the length of the first, expressed in formula.

Section of opposite tonal relation

After an introductory process maintaining the characteristic rhythm of the movement, the main tune is referred to in a 6-bar phrase in C minor, on the dark side of B flat, and this same material continues in a prolonged series of dark-side modulations, which themselves, from F minor to F minor, constitute a process of 'home (F minor)—bright (D flat major)—dark (E flat minor—G flat major-minor—G minor—C minor)—home (F minor)'.

The return to the first key is achieved by means of the opening material.

Dance movements, as has been mentioned in connection with the structures of Bach, exhibit the tonal principle under discussion as far back as the middle seventeenth century, and no doubt examples can be found even closer to the emergence of major–minor tonality.

In the second main structural element of this trio a purely thematic analysis might accuse the triple alternation of tunes and tonalities of squareness. But relative to the tonal basis of the structure it takes on the kind of closely wrought double meaning which seems to be one of Beethoven's main preoccupations in these late works.

The thematic scheme is *Aa : aBA aBA aB*. But the thematic subdivisions are constantly crossed by the tonal functions. Thus the first *aB* constitutes an introduction to the section of opposite relation, continuing the tonality of the second main key section (D flat major). The subsequent *A* (B flat minor) is in opposite relation and is followed by *aB* (G flat major) in the same function. *A* re-establishes the tonic, and the final *aB* (B flat major) acts as a cross between a coda and a link to the return of the scherzo. The thematic reiteration leads the listener to regard this as part of the trio; thus the omission of the expected final appearance of *A* creates the impression of an incomplete trio leading directly back to the scherzo (cf. p. 167), though the structure has in fact been both tonally and thematically completed at the conclusion of the previous *A*.

The interweaving of tonal and thematic functions may be shown in diagram thus:

Tonality:	First main key	Second main key	Section of opposite relation		Return of first key	Coda or link	
	E♭ mi	D♭ ma	D♭ ma	B♭ mi	G♭ ma	E♭ mi	B♭ ma
Themes:	*A*	*a*	*aB*	*A*	*aB*	*A*	*aB*

The effect is very much more complex in sound (which is what matters) than it looks on paper, and it would be 'Hats off', were they not off these seven-score years.

FOURTH MOVEMENT

Home key: E flat (after an introductory sensation of G minor), expressed in Ex. 38a.

Ex. 38

(a) BEETHOVEN: String Quartet No. 12 in E♭, op. 127 · 4th movement

Second main tonality: the dominant, on the bright side of the home key, expressed most decisively in Ex. 38b.

(b)

Section of opposite tonal relation

The third main tonal area begins with the C minor—E flat introductory process which had opened the movement and, after a transient modulation to F minor, moves to the dominant chord of that key on which it introduces, as if C major were already a key rather than a chord, the tune of the second main tonality. After completing its first four bars in that 'inappropriately' bright key, it plunges from the major mode into the minor for the beginning of the process of tonal opposition proper. This passes from C minor to F minor, introduces F major as if it were to be a facetious answer to the previous C major, and then lets it be known that, after all, it was introduced as the dominant chord of B flat. This key occurs not as a structural dominant but, like the tonic which soon after follows it, as part of a sequential process leading to the subdominant. Here appears what sounds like a 'false return' of the main theme—that is, sounding like a *structural* return, but not being one—including its second element, which has not been heard since the beginning (Ex. 38c).

(c)

The coda presents a new version of the movement's opening tune in a series of entries starting in C major, each a major 3rd below the last, after which the music returns to E flat to stay. Such coda-procedures have been called 'further development', but the frequent occurrence of wide modulation in Beethoven's larger codas does not in fact produce an effect comparable to that of the section of opposite tonal relation, even where that section is characterised by tonal diffusion. There is a true analogy in the reaction of a traveller to deflections of the road from his main line of advance. If, with the destination not yet in sight, the road veers widely from its expected direction, his state of mind towards the new turning will be different from his attitude to a *twist* in the road, however unexpected and however fascinating, when the destination is already visible. The first is an adventure of unpredictable proportions; the second an added pleasure in a sequence of events already almost completed. It is true that, presented with modulatory material and the question 'Is this from a "development" or a coda?', one would not know. But it is precisely the context which creates the difference of sensation, as it does in all structural functions.

Quartet in B flat major, Op. 130

FIRST MOVEMENT
Home key: B flat (introducing a good deal of its dominant) expressed in alternations of Ex. 39a,

Ex. 39

(a) BEETHOVEN: String Quartet No. 13 in B♭, op. 130 - 1st movement

Allegro ma non troppo

and

the second of which on its second appearance lasts for a considerable time and leads to a sleight-of-hand modulation from
the dominant note of the first key chromatically to the minor
3rd of the key, which then becomes, by virtue of what follows,
the dominant note of G flat major (Ex. 39b).

(b)

Beethoven then presents us with one of those cases in which
it is impossible—and therefore irrelevant—to decide at what
moment the second main tonal area, viewed structurally,
begins. For he plunges into G flat major, introduces a fragment
of tune, repeats the cello's process of plunge, very slightly
ornamented, and follows it with an extended version of the
'fragment of tune', allowing this to lead to new (but not very
new) material which arrives again at the dominant, but this
time the dominant 7th chord, of G flat major.

(c)

TMS—L

(d)

A version of the second tune of the first main tonal area then
follows (Ex. 39e),

(e)

and this may be considered 'the' tune of the second main tonal
area, or it may not, as the fancy of the listener prefers. It leads,
in the second ending of the repeated section, to the leading-note
of the key, and the third main tonal area begins with a process
of introduction in which G flat major, turned into F sharp
major for convenience of notation, continues as a process of
suspense. Having arrived at the tonic note, unharmonised, of
that key, it drops, still unharmonised, a major 3rd to D, which
is thereupon used as the tonic of the key of D, in a process
repeating the character of the preceding suspense, maintains
this sensation of suspense for seven more bars and then moves
to G major, the sub-dominant of D, as the main tonal element
of the section.

(f)

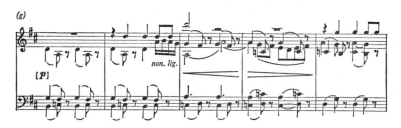

The subtlety of this series of tonal relationships remains astonishing however often it is heard. As we have seen, the second main key of the movement (G flat major) is reached abruptly from the initial B flat; the first key of the section of opposite relation—D major, another major third down—is reached even more abruptly from G flat (F sharp). If one tonal descent of a major third creates the sensation of the dark side of the original, another equal descent must duplicate the sensation. It does—but the surprise consists in that, immediately after one recognises a further descent to the dark side, there follows a most curious feeling of 'lift' in the realisation, as an apprehended fact of tonal experience, that the music is now on the bright side of the original key and therefore of the second key as well. Is there anyone but Beethoven who could wring out of tonal resources such a refinement as this? To Haydn and Mozart the utilisation of the material had not yet reached a stage which would drive them to such an extremity, and after Beethoven the interests of most composers turned elsewhere.

The return to B flat, otherwise rather abruptly achieved, is foreshadowed at the end of this section by five bars in the dark-side key of G minor which make the listener doubt whether the section of opposite relation is to continue.

The 21-bar coda, apart from three bars in G minor and C minor (one of which is really chromatically in B flat), remains entirely in the tonic.

THIRD MOVEMENT
Home key: D flat, expressed after a brief dominant-suspense introduction, as:

Ex. 40
(*a*) BEETHOVEN: String Quartet No. 13 in B♭, op. 130 - 3rd movement
Andante con moto, ma non troppo

The one-bar process of modulation to the dominant adds tongue-in-cheek to sleight-of-hand:

(*b*)

and the following tune

(*c*)

adds to the brightness of its A flat, in relation to D flat, by moving briefly but thematically decisively to C major and F major before returning dutifully to A flat for the completion of a thematic process which, all in all, is one of Beethoven's most touching expressions of serenity.

Section of opposite tonal relation
A standard Classical slow-movement procedure expresses the first and second main tonalities by means of lyrical tunes and may have either a section of opposite tonal relation or a sensation of suspense (sometimes very short—even, rarely, nothing at all) between the end of the second main tonal area and the structural return of the home key. (Traditionally, when there is no section of opposite tonal relation, the resulting structure is called 'modified sonata-form'. But neither is a modification of the other. They are both valid expressions of governing tonal principles.)

To insist on pigeon-holing every musical process is an infallible way of paralysing the capacity for aesthetic perception. Yet every piece of music must derive its shape from a principle governing the relationship of its parts, and we cannot appreciate —or even apprehend—subtleties until we have grasped the commonplace possibilities inherent in the operation of the parent principle. Commonplaces of procedure at this point of a classical lyric sonata-form include: a return to the tonic for the beginning of the section of opposite relation; a sensation of introduction at the beginning of the section; a sensation of suspense instead of it; and establishment of the dominant key shortly before the return of the tonic.

In this movement Beethoven uses or brings to mind all these with such delicacy that we are scarcely conscious of one before it has been superseded by another. The use of the tonic key which initiates the section of opposite relation grows from the last melodic element of the second main key section in such a way that it sounds like a sequential procedure still within that section, and these two bars with the following bar, modulating briefly to E flat minor and back to the tonic, at the same time suggest an introductory process to the main section of opposite relation. This itself, starting with another appearance of the same tune in the tonic, still continues the character of the second main key section, even though transposed.

The sequential process which now starts culminates in establishing the dominant key and this, even though the movement to the dark side (B flat minor and, by implication, E flat minor) is unmistakable in the context, suggests in retrospect that the approach to the dominant (whose own function is to reintroduce the tonic) has been implied ever since the start of the sequences. Furthermore, since a sequential process always throws the mind onward to the moment at which it will cease and forward motion be resumed, this section, besides its implication of the tonic's impending return, also creates within itself a sensation of suspense.

FOURTH MOVEMENT

This movement is not in sonata-form, but its procedures are influenced by the tonal principles of that structure. Its basic structure is that of a scherzo and trio. The scherzo is straightforward—if it can be called straightforward to combine innocence and experience in one miraculous song. The trio however puts three stumbling-blocks in the way of recognising its structural nature. First, its opening tune:

Ex. 41

BEETHOVEN: String Quartet No. 13 in B♭, op. 130 - 4th movement

(a)

is reminiscent of Haydn's coda-tunes and, being in the same key as the scherzo, will probably lead the hearer to decide he is listening to its coda; secondly, the repetition of that opening

tune is followed by two more statements of it in the subdominant (Ex. 41b).

Finally, it re-establishes its first key only at the return to the
scherzo.

Beethoven's use of an incomplete trio leading directly back
to the scherzo goes back to his early works, and Haydn had
used it before him, so there is nothing startling about that. The
point of interest lies in the tonal relations within the trio.

After the repetition of the first eight bars, the descent into
the subdominant suggests that, if the trio is to be a complete
unit based on the customary principle of opposite relation,
what follows will move to the bright side of C—and therefore
necessarily of G. Beethoven chooses however to turn the whole
trio into a dark-side element of the larger structure comprising
both scherzo and trio: a device which gives full effect to the
radiant simplicity of the chief tune on its reappearance.

The dance-form which chooses, among many alternatives, a
first structural element beginning and ending in the same key,
followed by dominant suspense or movement to the bright side
before the return to the original key, is a commonplace of
classical procedure and its relationship to movements based on
the principle of opposite relation is unmistakable though
subtle. Beethoven's choice of the dark side in this situation
is no more subversive than his use of it as the second main

tonality in the first movement; as we have seen, its function includes acting as a foil to the return of the first tune.

SIXTH MOVEMENT

There can be no doubt, a hundred and thirty years after the event, that the structure of the quartet as a whole requires the massive, spiritually and intellectually demanding Great Fugue for its completion. The three movements following the first, indescribably beautiful as they are, ravish rather than rouse, and the cavatina, enigmatic in its intense compression, raises emotional expectations which are passionately fulfilled in the fugue but are left unanswered by the substitute finale. Subjective hypotheses in such matters are always dangerous, but, as long as we recognise this apotheosis of the popular Viennese mind for the masterpiece it is, we may allow ourselves to suppose that Beethoven, one of his greatest works having been rejected, determined to satisfy and simultaneously to 'needle' his contemporary audience; and, having designed the needle, to create with it a work of tonal and thematic profundity worthy of his own stature.

The tonal materials are:

First tonal area: C minor B flat, expressed in Ex. 42a.

Ex. 42

(a) BEETHOVEN: String Quartet No. 13 in B♭, op. 130 - 6th movement

Second main tonality: the **bright-side** dominant of the key of the work, expressed in a series of thematic procedures none of which seem to claim the privilege of being regarded as 'the' tune of the second main tonal area (Ex. 42b).

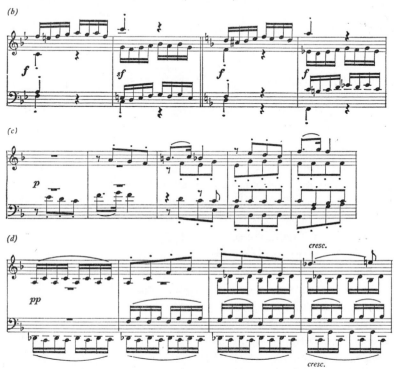

The first and third have too much the character of formula, and the second, though it comes nearest to the required definition of character, already sounds coda-like. The procedure represents therefore a deliberate sensation of uncertainty as to the moment at which the second main tonal area is to be recognised as starting: that sensation of which Haydn and Beethoven, of the three great Classicists, were particularly fond.

Section of opposite tonal relation
This consists of twelve bars of modulatory introduction, starting in the key of the second main tonal area and passing through

D minor and C minor to A flat—well on the dark side of F. In this key appears a forty-six-bar new tune which constitutes the main process of tonal opposition (Ex. 42e).

(e)

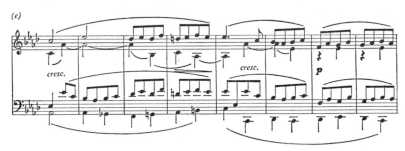

It is followed by material based on the opening tune of the movement, which first establishes the dominant of the home key and then moves through an extended process of modulation on the dark side, finishing on the dominant chord of the relative minor of the home key.

The tonal refinements of this movement are among the most delicate in Beethoven's extensive repertory. The opening tune itself has only twelve of its thirty-two bars in the tonality which it defines: a condition which prepares the way for the extreme (yet aurally apprehensible and comprehensible) subtlety of the return to the first tonality after the section of opposite relation. The opening tune is followed by fifty-eight bars of music in the dominant which twice—the first occasion lasting eight bars— casts doubt upon its intentions by reverting to the tonic. A modulatory introduction to the section of opposite relation then leads to fifty-one bars in A flat—well on the dark side— after which music in F minor, based on the opening tune, leads to a decisive appearance of F major in the character of the dominant. We are accustomed to this procedure—a bright-side key anticipating the return of the tonic—but we are not accustomed to having the process of anticipation last longer than the tonality of opposite relation and pass through a whole series of dark side keys as well as touching the tonic itself. Yet the dominant character of the use of F major is unmistakable and we become sure of this when thirty bars later the music settles into sixteen bars on the dominant chord of G minor—though we are not yet sure why it should be G minor.

This is clarified when the opening tune, having feinted in G minor to E flat, repeats itself in the original C minor to B flat and initiates the music re-establishing the first tonality.

The huge coda (157 bars) begins with a transposition, exact except for details, of the eight bars which had introduced the section of opposite tonal relation, followed by a transposed extension of the next four bars to eight. This leads to the first eight bars of the tune chiefly responsible for the sensation of opposite tonal relation in that section, now transposed to the corresponding key of E flat. The effect of such modulations in the coda has been discussed (p. 160). The tonality of B flat is then restored and maintained for seventy-six bars, when the key of C minor is briefly introduced in an appearance of the opening tune, C minor to B flat as at first. Thereafter for forty-six bars B flat unassailed, but for chromatic alterations.

BRAHMS' INSTRUMENTAL MUSIC

Tonal structure is dependent for its maximum efficiency on clear definition of keys, and therefore on relatively small amounts of chromaticism. There is plenty of chromaticism in the music of Haydn, Mozart and Beethoven, but they see to it that it occurs where the demands of structure can tolerate it, to be replaced by clear-cut key definition whenever it is structurally necessary.

Perhaps the most striking examples of this truth are to be found in Mozart's D major Minuet for piano (K. 355), in which the chromaticism of the first part of each main element of the structure is replaced by straightforward cadence formula when it becomes necessary to define the structure (Ex. 43), and in the same composer's almost atonal Gigue for piano (K. 574), where tonal stability is re-created at the appropriate points by means of pedal notes.

Ex. 43

Mozart: Minuet for Piano, K.355

Brahms, attempting to re-create the characteristics of classical structure in the mid-nineteenth century, was faced with the problem that the harmonic idiom had moved on. Just as twentieth-century composers find themselves forced into using the functions of the twelve-note scale, because major–minor tonality has, at least for now, been squeezed dry, so Brahms was forced by his own need for the tools of originality into using the chromatic and modulatory idiom of his time. Thus it is scarcely too much to say that in seeking to express classical structure in the Romantic idiom Brahms was attempting the impossible, and that therefore he failed. But a failure to achieve a theoretical intention is not necessarily a failure to achieve superlative works of art. Wagner, like Brahms, was a tonal structuralist and he solved his problem with success. But Brahms' problem was more serious, for as a symphonist he could not within the scope of his relatively short movements assert anything like—for example—the 374 bars of the tonality of B and its associates which finish Act II of *Tannhäuser*, without hopelessly overbalancing the structure of the whole.

Brahms' need, taking into account the chromatic and modulatory character of the idiom, was to provide himself with room for tonal ambiguity without undermining the classical foundations upon which he had determined. His solution as it appears in the symphonies is authentically classic in its simplicity.

We have seen that classical sonata-form is essentially a procedure of opposing tonal relationships, in which the relation between the third main tonal area and the second is the opposite of that which holds between the second and the first. We have seen that Mozart in particular was given to defining these tonal areas by means of one set of tunes for the first main tonal area and another set for the second. In some cases thematic development then followed, but the main function of the area in which that development occurred was to act as the 'section of opposite tonal relation'. This was most often on the dark side of the second main tonal area since the second had been on the bright side of the first.

Brahms wanted (whether consciously or not is irrelevant) the structural advantages of the process of opposite tonal relation, but he also wanted the advantage of freedom for the tonal ambiguity inherent in the chromatic Romantic idiom. He got out of his difficulty by bringing the section of opposite tonal relation (speaking *only* of its tonal aspect, not of its thematic character of development) forward as a second element of the second main tonal area. By this means he left the third main tonal area proper, which in his case is always also a thematic development, free for any amount of chromatic ambiguity or oscillation between bright and dark. He even has no objection to using it for further dark-side material if he is so inclined. The structural requirements of the movement, apart from the inevitable return to the tonic, having already been completed by the end of the now tonally subdivided second main tonal area, he feels tonally entirely free within the third.

In the C minor Symphony these procedures are worked out as follows. The material of the first main tonal area begins:

Ex. 44

(a) BRAHMS: Symphony No. 1 in C minor - 1st movement

and leads, after considerable chromatic modulation, to a cadence in the home key. Thence it moves by way of further modulation to the Classically most predictable key of the relative major, expressed thematically by material barely distinguishable from what has preceded it:

(b)

At the conclusion of this material Brahms plunges into the key of E flat minor with thematic material so strong that, in view of the relative thematic indistinguishability of the E flat major material, the minor mode of that key is apt to sound like the second main tonality itself, without the occurrence of any process of opposite tonal relation. As the slow movement of Beethoven's A minor quartet would not in itself have led to the establishment of the tonal principle behind his 'special' kind of variation form, but conforms to the principle more clearly established in other examples, so this movement of Brahms would not in itself have led to the formulation of the principle behind his sonata-form procedures in the symphonies. But in view of what we shall find clearly demonstrated in the last movement of the C minor Symphony and in a number of other movements, it can be seen to conform to that principle.

The E flat minor material, forming a process of opposite tonal relation with the preceding E flat major, which had been on the bright side of the home key, is:

(c)

Such a procedure was not quite new in Brahms. Beethoven had in perhaps a score of cases used a double-tonality unit for the second main tonal area: the dominant minor to its major, for example, in the first movement of the piano sonata Op. 2 No. 2, and the dominant preceded by its relative minor in the first movement of the Seventh Symphony. But he had apparently thought of it not as a strongly structural function, but merely as an ornamental factor. For the third main tonal area in such cases performs its usual function as a section of opposite tonal relation, though, in the context of one aspect of Brahms' view, this function has already been fulfilled.

Section of opposite tonal relation

In the Brahms movement under discussion the relationship between the third main tonal area (which is a true 'development section'—i.e., it exploits previously announced material) and the second tonal area takes up its option to be ambiguous, even though there is the briefest of moments right at the beginning of it when the E flat minor of the preceding section is followed by a bright C flat major (in the notation of B). There are so many alternations of bright and dark within it that it becomes quite impossible to establish a sensation which could serve as opposition of tonal relation with respect to the sensations of 'home', 'bright' and 'dark' which precede it.

We may note, however, that in the material which follows the structural return to the home key, the thematically rather 'faceless' material which had constituted the first part of the second main tonal area, in E flat major, receives considerable definition in retrospect by its return in C major, after the minor mode return of the first material, and before the minor mode coda.

FOURTH MOVEMENT
Home key: C major, expressed, after an extended C minor-major introduction, as

Ex. 45
(a) BRAHMS: Symphony No. 1 in C minor - 4th movement

After this tune has been repeated, the same sort of material continues, but animato, through an extended process of chromaticism and modulation which leads by way of an appearance of the introduction's horn-call to the second main tonality—the dominant—expressed as:

The process of opposite tonal relation again takes place within the second main tonal area, and is provided by movement, not to the tonic minor of the preceding key, as in the first movement, but to the relative minor. It is approached and left several times, alternating with a sensation of C major, and is finally very strongly established by a vigorous E minor cadence.

Here Brahms makes use of a device which, though he was especially fond of it, did not originate with him: that of establishing the structural return to the home key immediately after the second main tonal area. Obviously this happens in every Classical rondo. But there are movements in which the event takes place which do not sound like rondos, and one of them is to be found in the last movement of Haydn's E flat Symphony, No. 103. In that movement, the first tonal area is expressed as:

Ex. 46

(a) HAYDN: Symphony No. 103 in E♭ - 4th movement

in a tune which lasts altogether for sixty-nine bars.

The second main tonality is expressed by means of the same thematic process, somewhat differently treated:

after which the first twenty-five bars of the opening material return, finishing with a modulation to the relative minor in which a process of opposite tonal relation begins and, after considerable modulation in appropriate dark-side keys, ends. At its end, the opening theme is resumed, creating the sensation that the dark-side developmental procedure had been an interruption in a return to the home key which from its start had been structural and final.

The materials in which this procedure is carried out in the third main tonal area of the fourth movement of Brahms' C minor symphony are: (1) a complete statement of the opening tune of the movement, constituting, in Haydn's manner, the structural return to the home key; (2) a dark-side, developmental 'interruption'; (3) the resumption of the opening material at the point at which it left off:

Ex. 47

BRAHMS: Symphony No. 1 in C minor - 4th movement

We may note finally that the 'dark' character of the interruption is an example of Brahms' freedom to use the dark-side again if he wants to: the sensation of opposite tonal relation having already been provided by E minor after G, in the second main tonal area.

From the point of view of tonal analysis, the most interesting aspect of Brahms' Second Symphony is that it is the only one of the four in which he follows Classical procedures without introducing his own methods of re-working them. Thus it suggests strongly that Brahms recognised the factors in his own music which were and were not Classical without alteration.

It is easy to fall into the trap of imagining that such a statement implies some set of rules to which the composers concerned are supposed to have given 'their loving obedience' (Morris, quoting Rockstro). Since Morris we have, I trust, been aware that there are no rules: composers find the right way to say what they have to say. But to recognise this is not to deny that in some periods of musical experience the 'right way' has included, almost without being questioned because it was clearly the appropriate way for the purpose, certain basic procedures. It is such basic procedures that are here meant. Brahms 'knew' —whether cognitively or not is irrelevant—when he was bringing the process of tonal opposition forward into the second main tonal area and when he was not. In the Second Symphony he did not.

The first movement of the Third Symphony provides almost a handbook to the tonal possibilities discoverable within the framework of the implications of Classical sonata-form with one decision taken.

Its chief materials are as follows:

Home key: F major, expressed as:

Ex. 48

(a) BRAHMS: Symphony No. 3 in F - 1st movement

Second main tonal area: (1) A major, expressed as:

(b)

followed by:

(c)

(2) A minor, expressed as:

(d)

Brahms' decision to follow F major with A major as the second main tonality, and to follow that with its own minor as the process of tonal opposition within the second tonality, gives him, in addition to complete tonal freedom in the third structural element of the movement, the following possibilities—to mention only the ones he chose—for what would normally be the return to the home key.

(1) Since the Classically most predictable key for the second main tonality would have been C—the dominant of F—the reappearance of the thematic material of this tonal area, if it took place at all (as in Brahms it would be most likely to do), would take place in the subdominant of the key in which it first appeared—i.e., the tonic. Brahms, having chosen A (the brightest possible key in relation to F) for the second main tonality, was able to make a deadpan further decision to follow Classical procedure literally at the return of this material, and put it in the subdominant of A—namely, D major.

(2) We have seen that one of Brahms' fondnesses was for starting the return of previously heard material in the 'wrong' key, structurally speaking. Thus the transference of this material from D major to F major in its course is not only a structural necessity but a Brahmsian trade-mark.

(3) Having arrived 'home', the obvious thing to do now is to put the material that had followed A major in A minor into the tonic minor, as he had done in both the first and last movements of the First Symphony. But Brahms doesn't want to be obvious, so what are the alternatives? The evidence of his choice shows that he wants to keep this material in the minor mode; but the nearest minor for him to go to is not the tonic minor of F—which though it would preserve the same tonal centre would be very abruptly on the dark side of its major—but its 'relative' minor. So Brahms chooses the relative minor of the F major which has just been re-established, and in doing so re-establishes the tonality of D, which had preceded F and had just given place to what seemed likely to be the final return 'home'.

(4) But by now Brahms has reached the end of the materials

of the movement, and there is nothing for it, if the movement is ever to reach home at all, but to use the coda as the means of getting there. Which he does; and in doing so makes a small, not important, but enjoyable piece of musical history.

The fourth movement of this symphony makes use of both Brahms' methods of re-working Classical structure: the tonal method of bringing the process of tonal opposition forward into the second main tonal area, and the thematic method of interrupting a structural return of the opening material which begins immediately after the second main tonal area. Its main materials are:

Home Key: F minor, expressed as:

Ex. 49

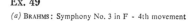

What we may call for convenience, quoting Robert Louis Stevenson in another context, 'a solemn music', in A flat:

followed by material based on the opening theme.

Second main tonal area (like Mozart, Brahms nearly always clearly defines thematically the start of the second tonality)— C (the dominant) major, expressed as:

C minor, expressed in a theme for full orchestra:

(d)

constituting the process of tonal opposition within the second main tonal area.

The third main structural element, which is again a true development section, largely based on the 'solemn music', is tonally ambiguous in relation to the preceding material and leads (as the solemn music had at first) to material based on the opening theme, continuing the structural return to the home key which had taken place, after a brief introductory process, at the beginning of the process of development.

In the first as well as the slow movement of his Fourth Symphony Brahms uses both the devices: tonal and thematic. The main material of the first movement is:

Home key: E minor, expressed as:

Ex. 50

(a) BRAHMS: Symphony No. 4 in E minor · Ist movement

Second main tonal area: (1) B minor, expressed as:

(b)

followed immediately by:

(c)

(2) B major, expressed as:

followed by:

That is to say the process of opposite tonal relation takes place in the standard Classical (and Baroque) manner for a movement in which a minor tonic is followed by its dominant minor as second main tonality. We have already noted (p. 81) that in such a case the standard procedure in both periods was to answer the sensation of minor-to-minor with the decisively bolder minor-to-major, and this is Brahms' procedure here. Here again, therefore, but rather slyly, he has achieved the sensation of opposition of tonal relation within the second main tonal area, so that the third main structural element of the movement can be, and is, tonally ambiguous in relation to what preceded it.

In the same movement Brahms uses the thematic device of beginning the third main structural element with a statement of part of the opening tune of the movement, in the home key, constituting thereby a sensation of structural return to that key. After the process of thematic development which follows and which we have noted is tonally ambiguous in relation to the keys which structurally preceded it, he achieves the completion of the structural return home by the method he used in the last movements of the first and third symphonies: picking up the opening material of the movement roughly at the point at which the process of development had interrupted it. But in this movement there is a further refinement. The process of 'picking up where he left off' is preceded by a disguised restatement of the first four bars of the nine bars of the opening tune which had preceded the process of development:

The rhythm is so much altered that the reference can easily be overlooked, and the disguise is thickened by the rhythmically-changed fragments of tune-references being combined with broken-chord material previously heard in a different context:

Thus the opening material, on its appearance at the beginning of the structural return to the home key, is in fact complete. But its disguised start is designed to suggest that it is not: that it is dependent for completeness on the statement of the first nine bars of it which had initiated the third main tonal area (and which incidentally, as the tonic minor following the dominant major, had provided, despite the general tonal ambiguity of the section in relation to the preceding keys, a supererogatory process of opposite tonal relation).

The slow movement also uses both the devices, but without the added refinement of the disguised re-entry. Its main materials are:

Home key: E major, spiced with Phrygian flavour, expressed as Ex. 51 *(a)*

BRAHMS: Symphony No. 4 in E minor - 2nd movement
   Andante moderato

Material based on the opening tune:

leads to a process of ornamented dominant suspense in the
dominant minor:

followed by an intensely expressive tune in the dominant major
constituting the second main tonality of the movement.

The structural return to the home key occurs at the beginning
of the third main structural element with the first ten bars of
the opening tune. What follows is a process of development in
dark-side keys, and it does not matter whether we regard it as
the process of opposite tonal relation, following on a tonic-
major to dominant-major home-to-bright-side relationship in
the first structural element—in which case we shall have rele-
gated the process of dominant suspense in the dominant minor
to a *mere* ornamental process of dominant suspense; or whether
we regard it as an *additional* process of tonal opposition, subsequent to one already completed by the dominant minor followed
by the dominant major.

The structural return, after this extended interruption, picks
up indeed at this process of dominant suspense, now inevitably
transferred to the tonic minor, to be followed by the expressive
tune previously heard in B major, now in the tonic major. The
only important difference between this movement and other
examples of the 'interrupted structural return' procedure is that
considerably more of the opening material is omitted after the

interruption: a situation the material can allow because the opening tune is an ABA structure—one which for obvious reasons can be and often is represented in a structural function by its first (or last) element only.

The fourth movement of this symphony is to be a passacaglia which will give no opportunities for the tonal ingenuities that Brahms was given to applying to sonata-form. He is clearly reluctant to let an opportunity slip by, so the third movement, which has the character of a scherzo, breaks away from the scherzo-and-trio structure to become a fully developed movement in sonata-form with Brahms' special thematic added attraction but without his tonal specialty.

Its main materials are:

Home key: C major (Ex. 52a).

Ex. 52

(a) Brahms: Symphony No. 4 in E minor - 3rd movement

Allegro giocoso

Second main tonality: G major (oddly touched with the flavour of the dominant chord of C), expressed as:

(b)

The third main structural element, after beginning with the first five bars of the opening tune as the structural return to the home key, moves to the dark side to provide the element of tonal opposition which is absent from the second main tonal area.

Since the chord, which becomes the key, of D flat is approached through the subdominant major and minor chords of C, it sounds very dark and remote indeed. But it turns out, after eight and a half bars, to have been only a Neapolitan procedure in the home key after all; and the dominant chord of that key having been arrived at the opening material storms in on the chord of E flat which had constituted the second half of bar 10 of the opening material, and which, taken without preparation from the dominant chord of C, makes an unforgettable connection.

PART III

The Principle of Progressive Tonality

PART III

The Principle of Progressive Tonality

The question poses itself: are we to make tonal relationships, of this sort or some sort, a *criterion* for a musical work of art in the period under discussion? Emphatically not. It may well be—and I think it is the case—that musical works of art in the major–minor idiom *invariably* have relationships between tonal centres as the basis of their design. It may even be—and I incline to this opinion—that all musical works of art, in any time and in any place, have relationships between tonal centres as the basis of their design. If that should prove to be the case, its being so would derive from a combination of the physical nature of musical materials and the nature of structure as a concept which will be discussed below. In the meantime it is better to keep our feet on the ground and confine ourselves to description.

The work of Carl Nielsen intensifies the question. For it is not only, even if chiefly, in dramatic music written to a text that the principle of interlocking structure is put into practice. Examples of it appear in instrumental music as well, both in the major–minor period and after the emergence of the twelve-note idioms, and to recognise them when they occur can save us from inventing new descriptions when old ones will do. Nielsen characteristically ends his works in keys other than those in which they began, and wherever this occurs we must, given our preceding findings, establish, before looking for any other hypothesis, whether the work concerned manifests an interlocking structure.

Such phenomena in Nielsen's music have been said to exhibit

what is called a 'principle of progressive tonality', defined no further than as a 'dynamic view of tonality (that a key is a starting-point for an expedition to another key) . . .', with the term 'tonality' clarified only by such references as to Nielsen's 'use of tonality as an evolving entity' and to his treatment of a chosen key 'as a goal to be achieved or an order to be evolved' (Robert Simpson, *Carl Nielsen, Symphonist*). Since the definition and its clarifications are clearly insufficient to establish the usefulness of the phrase, we must either arrive at a satisfactory definition of progressive tonality as a structural function, or abandon the concept.

MAHLER

The hypothesis is supported by reference to the music of Mahler, more than half of whose symphonies end in keys other than those in which they began. Picking at random among those that are so constructed we can use the Second and Seventh Symphonies to show that his procedures do not really establish a 'principle of progressive tonality'.

The Second Symphony is tonally constructed in the following way (see page 193).

The structure of this is clearly 'something-interlocking-with-C', the only trouble in deciding what the 'something' is, seeing that there are four contenders—not all of them very vigorous.

E major is the only tonality in the work which does *not* interlock with C, but is enclosed in it. It constitutes the second main tonal area of the first movement, reappearing both in the structural return of that movement's first material (contrary to classical procedure, but acceptably since the structure of the work is not by movements but overall) and in the middle section of the third movement.

A♭ contends fairly vigorously to be regarded as the main key interlocking with C, since it is the key of the second movement and the penultimate key of the work. Similarly D♭ is the key

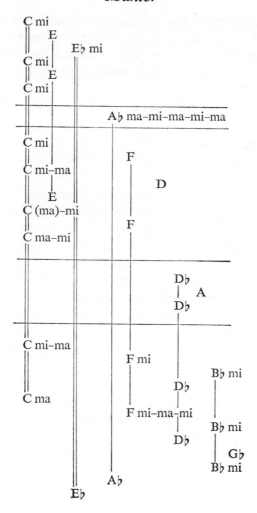

of the fourth movement and an antepenultimate key of the
work, and F is the subordinate key of the third movement and,
in its minor mode and interlocking with B♭ minor, an important
element in the last movement.

But there is always a strong case to be made for the tonality
which ends the work unless its previous absence excludes it from
consideration, and in this case the E♭ climax of the last move-

ment is amply prepared, as the closing element in the consequent of an interlocking structure, by the very strong appearance in E♭ minor of the opening material of the first movement, as the third main tonal area of that movement, after C minor and E major.

Mahler's Seventh Symphony, constructed tonally as shown on the opposite page, is essentially a work in C, but its first movement establishes an interlocking structure of B and E, with E predominating. In the course of the first structural appearance of E the key of C is decisively introduced ('mit grossem Schwung'), but not more decisively than several other tonalities which are ornamental in character—particularly the series of surprise modulations which precede the final appearance of C in the last movement. If we choose to regard this first appearance of C as structural we have an interlocking E/C structure overall, with B interlocking in a subsidiary sense with E. If we regard that appearance of C as ornamental, then the work is a large-scale C structure preceded by the interlocking structure of B/E; constituting a structure of juxtaposed tonalities—a type whose historical background we shall shortly have occasion to investigate.

In neither of these Mahler symphonies, therefore, have we been able to establish the need for a new category of musical structure to be called 'progressive tonality'—nor shall we be able to in any other of his works.

HINDEMITH

The music of Hindemith might perhaps be regarded as a promising prospect for progressive tonality. For he talked of 'organic structures' and was apt to make rude remarks about pre-set combinations (though, by an inconsistency only apparent, he insisted that each organic structure be pre-set).

But the symphonic suite derived from his opera *Mathis der*

Mahler—Seventh Symphony

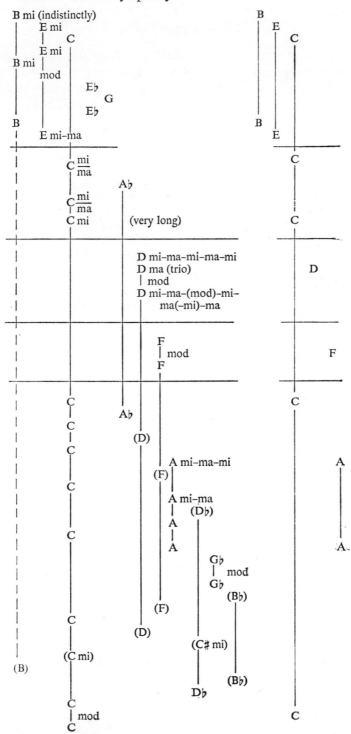

Maler is no progression of tonalities in this sense, but a particularly striking example of the interlocking principle at work in a tonal twentieth-century idiom: the more so as it applies to the opera as well as to the suite. The structural outline of the suite is as follows:

Hindemith—Suite from *Mathis der Maler*

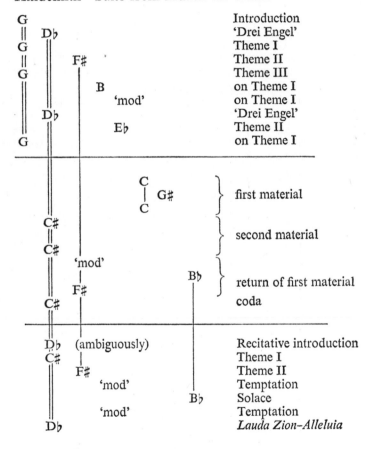

G ‖ G ‖ G ‖	Db		Introduction
			'Drei Engel'
			Theme I
	F♯		Theme II
			Theme III
	B		on Theme I
		'mod'	on Theme I
	Db		'Drei Engel'
	Eb		Theme II
G			on Theme I

C ｜ G♯   first material
C

C♯ ‖ C♯   second material

'mod'   Bb   return of first material

C♯ ‖ F♯   coda

Db (ambiguously)   Recitative introduction
C♯   Theme I
     F♯   Theme II
     'mod'   Temptation
           Bb   Solace
     'mod'   Temptation
Db   *Lauda Zion–Alleluia*

The slow movement, taken by itself, *looks* on paper as though it ought to be a C♯ movement with a C-natural introduction. But because of its thematic nature and its proportions it is very difficult to accept it as such when we hear it. To recognise the work overall as an interlocking G/Db structure enables us also to recognise that the C—G♯—C structure at the beginning of the slow movement is ornamental to the main interlocking process of the work, and does not need to be accounted for within the slow movement taken separately—a movement which, in the opera, has the structural C♯ function of bringing the work to its close, ending the Db/C♯ element which interlocks with G to constitute the total structure.

Hindemith recognised four important tonal functions in relation to any tonal centre: the dominant, the subdominant, and the upper and lower leading-notes. The tonal relationships of the *Mathis* suite are therefore interesting as a set of fingerprints.

It begins with a closed G structure constituting the first movement. The ornamental C structure which starts the second movement is the subdominant of G—but it is also the lower leading-note of C♯, with which the G structure interlocks as the main outline of the work. The rather unexpected tonality of G♯, the middle section of the C structure, is the upper leading-note of G as well as the dominant of C♯. The 'second main tonal areas' in both the first and last movements are on the tonal centre of F♯, the subdominant of C♯ and the lower leading-note of G.

Finally we may note that the C♯ structure which begins in the second movement is tonally a mirror:

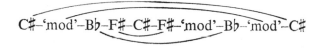

C♯–'mod'–Bb–F♯–C♯–F♯–'mod'–Bb–'mod'–C♯

So far then, in the cited examples of music by Richard Strauss, (see pages 72–3), Mahler and Hindemith, we have found no precedent for the proposed 'principle of progressive tonality'. But something that might be regarded as a precedent crops up in a most unexpected place.

MOZART

There are three Mozart operas which are neither closed tonal structures, ending where they began, nor interlocking structures. (The only one of the latter sort in the whole series is *Zaïde*, written in 1780.)

As to *Apollo et Hyacinthus* (K.38, 1766), it would be easy to take refuge in the remark that one doesn't expect much structural sense from a ten-year-old.

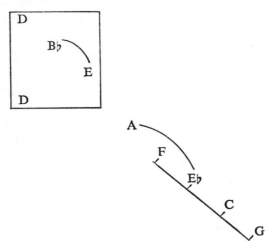

But, in addition to the fact that one cannot safely make statements about what one can 'expect' of a Mozart, the diagrams of *L'Oca del Cairo* (K. 422, 1783):

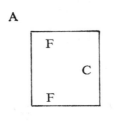

Eb

Bb

and *Lo Sposo deluso* (K. 430, 1783):

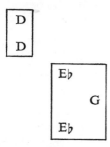

though they are less disturbing to a tonal theory of dramatic-musical structure, forbid so easy a solution.

What can we say that is structurally true about all three cases? There is in each of them at least not less than one 'symmetrical' structure, flanked by other keys. In the case of *Apollo et Hyacinthus* these other keys occur *after* the symmetrical structure with which the opera begins, and they do not present any obvious structural relationships, either with each other or with the D structure. The D structure at the beginning contains two tonalities only, at the interval of the augmented 4th—B♭ and E, and this procedure is answered after the conclusion of the D structure by tonalities at the same interval—A and E♭—interlocking with a series of three keys each a perfect 4th apart—F, C and G.

The juxtaposition of A and E♭ has in fact an interesting—though probably structurally insignificant—history in the operas of Mozart. It appears in *Il Sogno di Scipione* (K. 126, 1772), *Lucio Silla* (K. 135, 1772), *La Finta Giardiniera* (K. 196, 1774)—twice—*Il Re pastore* (K. 208, 1775)—twice—*Zaïde* (K. 344, 1780), *Idomeneo* (K. 366, 1781)—twice—*Die Entführung aus dem Serail* (K. 384, 1782), *L'Oca del Cairo* (K. 422, 1783) and *La Clemenza di Tito* (K. 621, 1791). At the least, one is inclined to regard it as a subjective and probably unconscious preference of Mozart's. Whether this in itself would enable him to regard the use of it to balance another augmented 4th relationship as adequate to the function of a structural pillar in *Apollo et*

Hyacinthus is the question, and one which I do not pretend to answer. It is, I think, fair—since he never did such a thing again—to emphasise that he was ten.

The case of *L'Oca del Cairo* is easier, especially in view of the re-appearance there of the A/E♭ relationship. The two keys here enclose a symmetrical F—C—F structure, and the E♭ is followed by its dominant as the concluding tonality of the opera. Especially in so short a work one has, I think, no difficulty in accepting this as a comprehensible structure. *Lo Sposo deluso* is even more accommodating in that, though it ends elsewhere than it began, and is not an interlocking structure, it simply juxtaposes two closed structures, D and E♭—G—E♭.

Thus we have Mozart's assurance that if the work is small enough—for one must not lose sight of the fact that *all* Mozart's other operas are closed tonal structures, from *Bastien und Bastienne*, written when he was twelve, and *La Finta Semplice*, a full-length opera written that same summer, to *Die Zauberflöte* and *La Clemenza di Tito*—there is no objection to mere juxtaposition of keys as a structural function, as long as there is at least one 'symmetrical' structure to relate them to, and some comprehensibility of relation among the juxtaposed keys. That is to say, in the case of small works we must broaden our definition of what constitutes a comprehensible structure to include what we may consent to call a very limited sort of 'progressive tonality', in which some tonal patterns are yet discernible.

NIELSEN

Our question concerning the structure of Nielsen's music then becomes: do these procedures of Mozart's constitute a precedent for Nielsen? Do Nielsen's structures show comparable, even though not in the same sense symmetrical, internal relationships? If not, does his music bring into being new structures, equally or acceptably comprehensible? In the latter case we shall have to establish some criteria for 'acceptable comprehensibility', and therefore of the meaning we wish to give to the word 'structure' itself.

An attempt to bring this word to a firm definition applicable to all disciplines discovers, as was discovered at a symposium held on the subject in Paris in 1965, that very wide differences occur in the accepted uses of the term. For our purpose it will suffice to accept Eddington's definition, Kantian in essence, that structure is a concept imposed by the mind of its own necessity on its experiences: that it is the mind's subjective reduction to comprehensibility of its experience of objective reality, and that without this subjectively imposed structure there is no comprehension. In practice this means that facts of experience (including 'ideas', in the sense of imagined concepts) give rise to a structural hypothesis; the hypothesis proves 'usable', in that it collects around itself other facts of experiences to which it validly refers; from these experiences another hypothesis can be put forward; and so on.

So it is with the structure of a work of art. The artist starts from an 'urge to create' which contains in it facts of his experience *as an artist*: some perhaps clear-cut, some likely to be very cloudy, all of them relevant to the series of steps, comparable to those of the hypothesising scientist, which he takes to bring his initial 'idea' into a state of untranslatable but communicable 'logic'. The scientist checks his hypothesis by whether it works in the context for which he needs it. The artist checks his structural steps by whether they work in the context of the demands made by his initial idea.

Thus in works of art as in works of science, a specific 'structure' is what results from forging a chain of deductively interdependent concepts: a chain which can figuratively be said to 'hold together' something that 'works'. Given that without the mind's subjectively imposed structure there is no comprehension, it follows that conversely something that works—which in a work of art means 'is comprehensible' as a prerequisite to 'is expressive'—is structured (though not necessarily that if it does *not* work it is unstructured or badly structured: it may be mechanically faultless, and inexpressive).

As to Nielsen, we may agree, without entering upon a discussion of his ultimate importance in musical history, that his music 'works'—that is, it is both comprehensible and expressive. But what methods does he use to achieve structural comprehensibility?

We shall find that he, like others before him, used the principle of interlocking tonal structure, but used it in a manner sufficiently veiled to give an initial impression of mere juxtaposition of tonalities. He also used a principle which we may call that of 'close tonal relation', in which the closing key of a work, though it is neither the opening key nor one that interlocks with it, is closely related to it. Where this occurs the procedure has a character in relation to the total structure comparable to the frequent appearance of operatic and oratorio preludes which are in keys other than the main key or keys of the work (for example, *Messiah*, with its overture and opening elements in E minor to E major, leading to the main tonality of D through its dominant), and even more directly related to the procedure found in *Aida*, which subsides after the conclusion of its second main (interlocking) tonality of D♭ major into G♭.

Nielsen's Second Symphony (*The Four Temperaments*) will serve as an example of such procedures (see page 203).

Clearly this is definable more specifically than by so generalised a term as 'progressive tonality'. The final key of A is the dominant of the relative major of the opening key of B minor, and D comes back importantly in the last movement. But what is more important is that the second main tonality of the first movement is G major, approached from D. The whole of the second movement is a G structure, with C major as its second main tonality. And the move to the final A major in the last movement is made through G followed by C (minor to major). If this appearance of G can be held to be structural rather than ornamental we have an interlocking B minor/G major structure, and this is a question on which there will certainly be difference of opinion. For the tonality of G major lasts for only thirteen bars (if we exclude the first two bars of the Adagio molto which also express a chromaticised G). This taken in

Nielsen—Symphony No. 2 (*The Four Temperaments*)

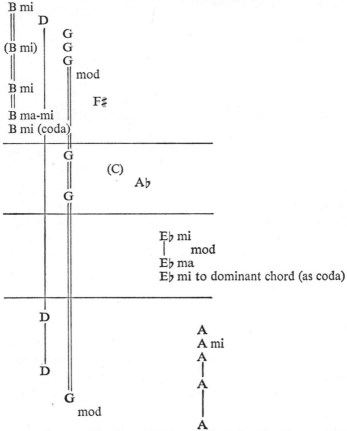

itself would incline one to reject it as a structural function. But those thirteen bars consist solely of *fff* reiterations of the tonic chord of G major. Why G major? It is at least arguable that it is so precisely because the composer, consciously or unconsciously, wanted the resulting overall interlocking structure, B minor/G major.

But suppose the suggested structural function of that key is rejected. It might also be held—though not, I think, with quite such strong factual support—that the interlocking structure is B minor/D major. For the first G major structure is preceded by five bars in D whose shortness might be held to be compensated by the lilting vigour of their tune:

Ex. 53

etc. 3 times

If this suggestion is in turn rejected—and I should myself reject it, though it may be worth noticing, in terms of the previous analysis, that the five bars of D are preceded by four bars of G minor—we still have, incontrovertibly, a structure consisting of B minor and G interlocking, followed by a self-contained tonality of E♭ (another major 3rd below the previous tonality, as G had been below B), followed by the relative major of B minor to its dominant: a far cry, surely, from the faceless generalisation of 'progressive tonality'.

Nor is such a generalisation supported by the structure of the *Sinfonia Espansiva* (see page 205).

The work is in fact an interlocking D/B♭ structure, in which the key of D has associated with it on two important appearances the key of A, its dominant, and in which the key of B♭ (usually minor) has associated with it several times the key of C♯ minor. E♭ (major to minor) forms an important internal constituent of the D structure, associated all except once with A♭. In the second and third movements combined, this association of A♭ and E♭ emerges as a reversing-end structure A♭—E♭/E♭—A♭, and it is noteworthy—though we may not wish to make very much of it—that this A♭ structure is bounded at the beginning of the second movement by the C minor material which follows A minor as a part of the transition from the

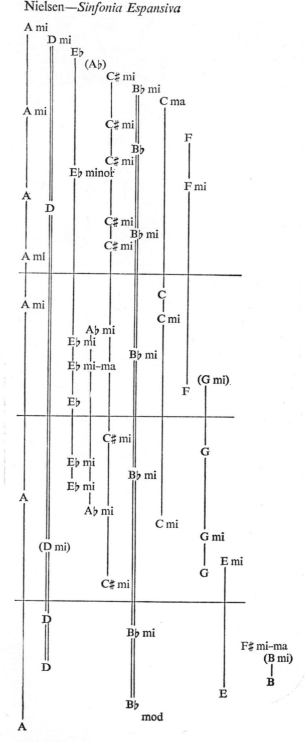

Nielsen—*Symphonies*

No. 1—G minor

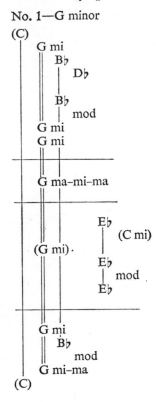

(C)

G mi

　　B♭

　　　　D♭

　　B♭

　　　mod

G mi

G mi

G ma–mi–ma

　　　　　E♭

　　　　　│　(C mi)

(G mi) ·

　　　　　E♭

　　　　　│　mod

　　　　　E♭

G mi

　B♭

　　　mod

G mi–ma

(C)

No. 4—*Inextinguishable*

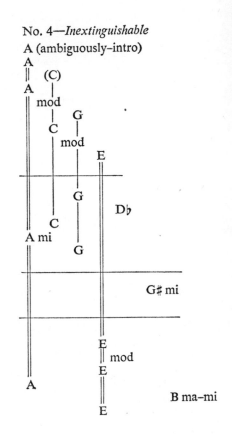

A (ambiguously–intro)

A

║　(C)

A

║　mod

　　　G

　　C

　　│　mod

　　　　　E

　　　　G

　　　　│

　　　　　　D♭

　　　C

A mi

　　　G

　　　　　　　　G♯ mi

　　　　　E

　　　　║　mod

　　　　E

A

　　　　║

　　　　　　　　B ma–mi

　　　　E

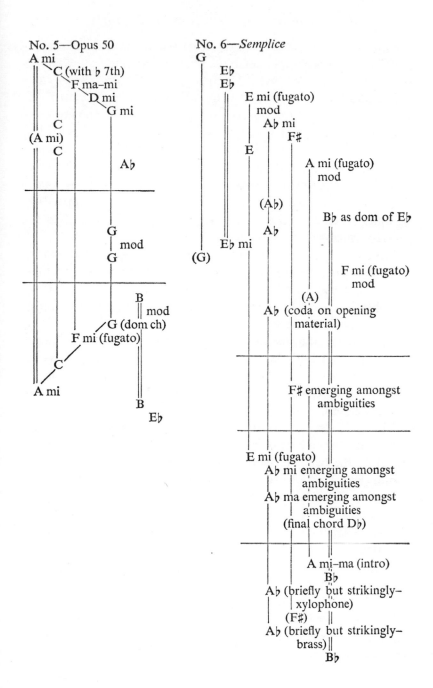

No. 5—Opus 50
A mi
C (with ♭ 7th)
F ma–mi
D mi
G mi
C
(A mi)
C
A♭
G
mod
G
B
mod
G (dom ch)
F mi (fugato)
C
A mi
B
E♭

No. 6—*Semplice*
G
E♭
E♭
E mi (fugato)
mod
A♭ mi
F♯
E
A mi (fugato)
mod
(A♭)
B♭ as dom of E♭
A♭
(G)
E♭ mi
F mi (fugato)
mod
(A)
A♭ (coda on opening
material)

F♯ emerging amongst
ambiguities

E mi (fugato)
A♭ mi emerging amongst
ambiguities
A♭ ma emerging amongst
ambiguities
(final chord D♭)

A mi–ma (intro)
B♭
A♭ (briefly but strikingly–
xylophone)
(F♯)
A♭ (briefly but strikingly–
brass)
B♭

opening C major to the E♭ re-appearance of the C major tune; and that C minor re-appears in the third movement, immediately upon the conclusion of the A♭ structure, as the first tonality of the fugato that leads by a modulating process to the return of C♯ minor to close the movement as it opened it. The importance of the tonality of C in this symphony can indeed hardly be overlooked in view of the vigorous 58 bars of material with which it concludes the first main structural element of the first movement, answering it with the opening tune of the second.

The remaining symphonies of Nielsen are equally amenable to more specific tonal analysis than the generalisation of 'progressive tonality' (see pages 206–7).

No 1 is G minor, framed in a modal C; No 4 an interlocking structure A/E. No 5 is an A minor structure, strongly mirror-like in character (A minor—C—F—G answered by G—F—C—A minor), interlocking with a B structure defined not only tonally but thematically.

The process of following a mirror structure with one or more as it were 'pendant' interlocking structures is nothing new. It appears more than once in the dramatic music of Handel, whose *Sosarme* is an example peculiarly clear and peculiarly complex (see page 209).

The main structure of the work is an interlocking D/F structure. But one can hardly fail to notice the mirror process extending from the overture to the end of the second Act: A—D—F minor/E♭—E minor—G minor—B♭ answered by B♭—G minor-to-major—E major—F minor/E♭—D—A. The key of B major in which Elmira sings her first aria, 'Rendi'l sereno al ciglio', is an interpolation in the mirror-structure, having as its structural function the provision of the bright-side element of the D structure which occupies most of Act I and which has as its dark third tonal area the remaining keys of F minor, E♭, E minor, G minor and C minor. It is notable also that the tonality of B♭ which constitutes the middle of the mirror has as *its* middle material the two main keys of the work—D and F—and that with this appearance of D there is associated the minor

Handel—*Sosarme*

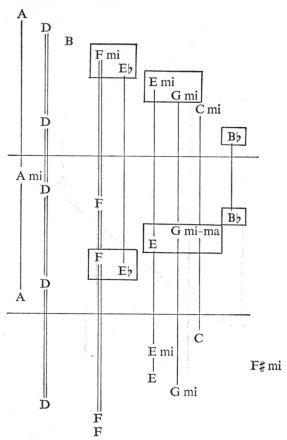

mode of the key of A which accompanies three of the five appearances of D in the opera.

Here there are no less than five 'pendant' interlocking structures. The key of D is extended beyond its mirror-structure function, and so are the keys of F, E minor–major, and G minor. Furthermore the 'independent' key of C (minor on its first appearance, major on its second) acts also in this capacity.

The tonal procedures of *Sosarme* constitute in fact a double mirror structure by reason of pendant interlocking structures (see page 210).

Handel—*Sosarme*

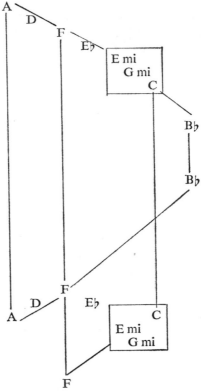

The first mirror-structure in this opera is, as we have seen, inescapably clear, in that the constituent keys of its consequent proceed in the reverse order of their original appearance. It is not always so. Sometimes the mirror, though unmistakably present, is 'blurred' because the keys of the consequent, though the same keys as those of the antecedent, appear in apparently random order. Handel's *Joshua* provides an example (see page 211).

We are aware that in some shadowy sense the keys which proceed from the beginning to the first appearance of D major are in general those which proceed from the beginning of Part II to the first tonality of Part III, and that the keys from the

Handel—*Joshua*

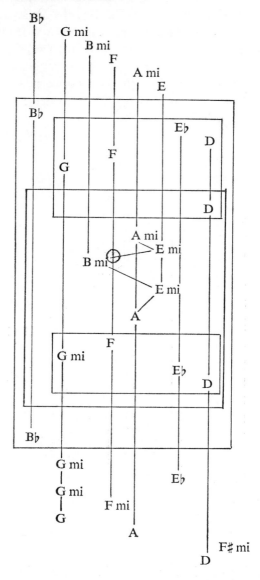

second appearance of B♭ to the third constitute an almost
exact mirror: B♭—E♭/D—F/G—(D)/A minor—E minor—

B minor, answered with B minor as the centre, by B minor—
E minor—A major—F/G—Eb/D—Bb. But as soon as we try
to bring the G minor, B minor, F, A minor and E major which
precede the second appearance of Bb into relation with the
larger mirror whose presence we seem to recognise by 'hunch',
we run into the difficulty that the keys concerned, though they
are the right keys, appear in two different orders:

Handel—*Joshua*

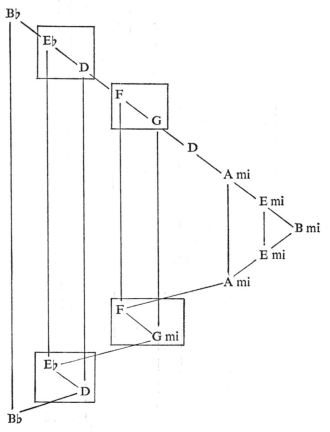

(placing the keys of the consequent in reverse order for clarity of
comparison).

All the keys are accounted for as being the same, and the

fact that they *are* the same needs in its turn to be accounted for, but we cannot quite call the total result a satisfactory example of a mirror. The alternatives seem to be either that 'the master's sense of form and logic' was satisfied by this shadowy pseudo-reverse presentation of the previously announced keys, or that Handel (in the case under discussion) did not intend the mirror procedure to extend beyond the area from the second B♭ to the third, and that the congruence between the key procedures of the first and last parts of the oratorio is designed:

Handel—*Joshua*

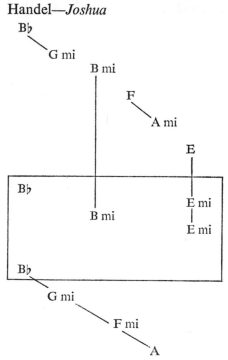

(The 'box' indicating the B♭ mirror previously described.)

F♯ minor, the only remaining key to be accounted for, presents no problem, acting as a process of return to the 'second main key' of D. (Is it quite incidental that the key chosen for this purpose is the dominant of B minor?—cf. *Sosarme*.)

Nielsen's Fifth Symphony adds a coda which is on the tonal

centre a major 3rd above B, as the final material of the first movement was on the tonal centre a major 3rd below C.

The Sixth Symphony interlocks G, E♭, A♭, F♯ and B♭, and one could have a field-day pitting analyst against analyst as to which interlocking process constitutes the main structure of the work. E♭ interlocking with B♭ seems the most likely contender, with G interlocking with E♭ in the familiar manner of preludes-not-in-the-main-key, and F♯ interlocking with both E♭ and B♭ ornamentally.

On the other hand, A♭ is curiously persistent in its misty way . . .

CONCLUSION

So much concentration on the tonal aspect of musical structure may strike the reader as over-simplification. It may seem ludicrous, for example, to reduce the splendours of Beethoven's *Missa Solemnis* to a diagram containing less than a score of keys: themselves reducible, with chromatic procedures and modulatory processes set aside, to five:

Beethoven — *Missa Solemnis*

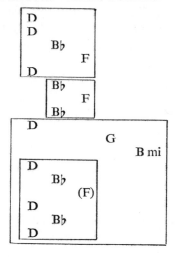

'Kyrie'
'Gloria in excelsis Deo'
'Gratias agimus'
'Domine Deus'
'Qui tollis'
'Credo in unum Deum'
'Et ascendit in coelum'
'Et vitam venturi'
Sanctus and Osanna
'Benedictus qui venit'
'Agnus Dei'
'Dona nobis pacem'
'Agnus Dei'
'Dona nobis pacem'
'Dona nobis pacem'
'Agnus Dei'
'Dona nobis pacem'

But man's power, it has been asserted, to comprehend a structure of any sort—not merely musical—depends on his capacity to reduce the analysis of that structure to expression in a few terms. Those few terms, if they are the right ones, describe the foundation of the structure. What has been attempted here is to strip away those elements of musical design which—rightly in the aesthetic context—seduce the mind from consideration of the foundations.

Eduard Hanslick has been vilified enough, and often un-justly, by Wagner-lovers. But he provides at the end of his pre-face to the seventh edition of *Vom Musikalisch-Schönen* a classic example of the result of paying attention to the wrong things first in musical analysis. He says: 'Since Liszt, the world has been enriched by Richard Wagner's doctrine of "infinite melody", i.e., formlessness exalted into a principle.' There could be no clearer statement of the nineteenth-century view, which has dominated much analytical thinking about music in the twentieth century and seems now likely to be also 'exalted into a principle': that musical forms are made of themes.

That tunes, harmonies and rhythms play an important part in music is self-evident. But these materials have to be shaped into a *piece* of music, and this shaping is—at any rate between 1600 and 1900, and I should be prepared to argue that the principle would apply much more widely, both in time and place —a matter of tonality.

I do not imply the over-simplification which often bedevils an already difficult problem: that 'form' is a sort of receptacle into which 'the music' is poured. Hanslick disposed of that idea, presumably for ever.

Form and music are one. There is no 'content' separable from the musical materials. There is no 'form' separable from the musical materials. There is no 'content' separable from the form, nor 'form' separable from the content.

Yet some factors in the musical material are especially func-tional in respect to consciously recognisable form.

Tonality does not monopolise this function. But it dominates it.

BIBLIOGRAPHY

(Restricted to works and books having direct relevance to the theories propounded in this book.)

A. MUSICAL WORKS

Bach, J. S.
Brandenburg Concertos 1–6
Concerto for two Violins and String Orchestra D minor
Concerto for Violin and String Orchestra E major
Orchestral Suites 1–4
Sonata for Flute and Harpischord E-flat
Das wohltemperiertes Klavier I, II
Die Kunst der Fuge
St Matthew Passion
St John Passion
Hohe Messe
Cantata No. 140—*Wachet auf, ruft uns die Stimme*

Beethoven, L. van
Sonatas for Violin and Piano 1–10
Sonatas for Piano 1–32
Symphonies 1–9
Concertos for Piano and Orchestra 1–5
Concerto for Violin and Orchestra Op. 61
Concerto for Violin, Cello and Piano Op. 56
String Quartets 1–16
Fidelio

Berlioz, Hector	*Symphonie Fantastique*
	Harold en Italie
	La Damnation de Faust
Brahms, Johannes	Symphonies 1–4
	Concertos for Piano and Orchestra 1 & 2
	Concerto for Violin and Orchestra
	Concerto for Violin, Cello and Orchestra
	Academic Festival Overture
	Chamber Music
Britten, Benjamin	*The Turn of the Screw*
Buxtehude, Dietrich	Keyboard works
Chopin, Frédéric	Concertos for Piano and Orchestra
Corelli, Arcangelo	*Concerti grossi*
Couperin, François	Keyboard works
Frescobaldi, G.	Keyboard works
Froberger, J. J.	Keyboard works
Gluck, C. W. von	*Orfeo ed Euridice*
Handel, G. F.	*Concerti grossi* 1–12, Op. 6
	Operas: *Ezio*
	Sosarme
	Ariodante
	Serse
	Oratorios: *Messiah*
	Judas Maccabaeus
	Joshua
	Solomon
	Jephtha

Haydn, F. J.   Symphonies: Nos. 1, 6, 7, 8, 13, 21,
                                    28, 31, 34, 36, 38, 42, 44,
                                    47, 48, 49, 52, 56, 64, 77,
                                    78, 82, 84, 85, 88, 91, 92,
                                    93, 94, 97, 98, 99, 100,
                                    101, 102, 103, 104
                          The Creation

Hindemith, Paul   Symphonic Suite: *Mathis der Maler*
                          Nobilissima Visione
                          The Four Temperaments
                          Symphony in E flat
                          String Quartets 1–7
                          Sonata for Violin and Piano in C, 1940
                          Sonata for Flute and Piano
                          Konzertmusik for Brass and Strings

Liszt, Franz   *Ce qu'on entend sur la montagne*
                          Tasso, Lamento e Trionfo
                          Les Préludes
                          Orpheus
                          Mazeppa
                          Hunnenschlacht

Lully, J.-B.   *Les Plaisirs de l'Isle Enchantée*
                          Le Bourgeois Gentilhomme
                          Grand Divertissement Royal
                          Monsieur de Pourceaugnac
                          Cadmus et Hermione
                          Alceste
                          Amadis de Gaule

Mahler, Gustav   Symphonies 1–9
                          Das Lied von der Erde

Mendelssohn, Felix	Symphony No. 4 in A minor Concertos for Piano and Orchestra Nos. 1 & 2 Concerto for Violin and Orchestra
Monteverdi, Claudio	*Orfeo*
Mozart, W. A.	Symphonies: G minor, K.183 D major (Haffner) K.385 C major, K.338 C major (Linz), K.425 E-flat major, K.543 G minor, K.550 C major, K.551

Concertos for Piano and Orchestra:
A major K.414
G major K.453
D minor K.466
A major K.488
C minor K.491
C major K.503
D major K.537
B-flat major K.595
Concertos for Violin and Orchestra:
D major K.218
A major K.219
String Quintets: C major K.515
G minor K.516
D major K.593
E-flat major K.614
Eine kleine Nachtmusik
Operas: *Idomeneo*
Le Nozze di Figaro
Don Giovanni
Così fan tutte
Die Zauberflöte

Purcell, Henry	*Dido and Aeneas*
	Keyboard works
	String Fantasias
Rameau, Jean-Philippe	Keyboard works
Scarlatti, Alessandro	*La Rosaura*
Scarlatti, Domenico	Keyboard works
Smetana, Frederick	*The Bartered Bride*
Strauss, Richard	*Der Rosenkavalier*
	Tone-poems: *Don Juan*
	Tod und Verklärung
	Till Eulenspiegel
	Also sprach Zarathustra
Stravinsky, Igor	Symphony in C (1945)
	Symphony in Three Movements
	Sonata for Two Pianos
Tchaikowsky, P. I.	Symphonies 1–6
Verdi, Giuseppi	*Rigoletto*
	Il Trovatore
	La Traviata
	La Forza del Destino
	Aida
	Otello
	Falstaff
Vivaldi, Antonio	Concertos
Wagner, Richard	*Der fliegende Holländer*
	Lohengrin
	Tannhäuser
	Tristan und Isolde
	Die Meistersinger von Nürnberg

Wagner, Richard   *Der Ring des Nibelungen:*
(*cont.*)   *Das Rheingold*
                         Die Walküre
                         Siegfried
                         Götterdämmerung
                         Parsifal

B. BOOKS

Apthorp, W. F.   *Opera, Past and Present*, London, 1901.
Bairstow, E.   *Handel's Oratorio, 'Messiah'*, London, 1928.

Barford, P.   *C.P.E. Bach*, London, 1964.
Bekker, P.   *The Changing Opera*, London, 1936.
Biron, F.   *Le Chant grégorien*, Ottawa, 1941.
Cardus, N.   *Mahler, His Mind and Music*, London, 1965.

Carrell, N.   *The Brandenburg Concertos*, London, 1963.

Cockshoot, J. V.   *The Fugue in the Piano Sonatas of Beethoven*, London, 1959.

Cooke, D.   *The Language of Music*, London, 1959.
Crosten, W. L.   *Grand Opera*, New York, 1948.
Dean, W.   *Handel's Oratorios and Masques*, London, 1959.

Del Mar, N.   *Richard Strauss*, Vol. I, London, 1962.
Demuth, N.   *French Opera*, London, 1963.
Dent, E. J.   *The Foundations of English Opera*, London, 1928
                    Mozart's Operas, London, 1913.

Dickinson, A. E. F. *The Musical Design of 'The Ring'*, London, 1926.

Donington, R.   *Wagner's 'Ring' and its Symbols*, London, 1963.

Einstein, A.   *Mozart*, London, 1945.
Ferretti, P.   *Esthétique grégorienne*, Paris, 1938.
Fontaine, P. H.   *Basic Formal Structures*, New York, 1967.

Green, D. M.	*Form in Tonal Music*, New York, 1965.
Grout, D.	*A Short History of Opera*, New York, 1947.
Hadow, H.	*Sonata Form*, 1896 and reprints.
Hopkins, A.	*Talking about Concertos*, London, 1964.
	Talking about Symphonies, London, 1961.
Hutchings, A.	*A Companion to Mozart's Piano Concertos*, London, 1948.
	The Baroque Concerto, London, 1961.
Kirkpatrick, R.	*Domenico Scarlatti*, New York, 1953.
Levarie, S.	*Mozart*, New York, 1962.
Loewenberg, A.	*Annals of Opera*, Cambridge, 1943.
Lootens, L.	*La Théorie musicale du Chant grégorien*, Paris, 1895.
Lorenz, A.	*Das Geheimnis der Form bei Richard Wagner*, Berlin, 1924–31.
Mahaim, I.	*Beethoven: Naissance et Renaissance des derniers Quatuors*, Paris, 1964.
Mann, W. S.	*Strauss: a Critical Study of the Operas*, London, 1964.
Martin, G.	*Verdi*, New York, 1963.
Mellers, W.	*The Sonata Principle*, London, 1957.
Mitchell, D.	*Gustav Mahler, The Early Years*, London, 1958.
Mocqereau, A.	*Le nombre musical grégorien*, Rome, 1908.
Moore, D.	*From Madrigal to Modern Music*, New York, 1942.
Morris, R. O.	*The Structure of Music*, London, 1935.
Newman, E.	*Gluck and the Opera*, London, 1895.
	Richard Wagner, London, 1933–47.
	Wagner as Man and Artist (2nd edn), London, 1924.
Oldroyd, G.	*The Technique and Spirit of Fugue*, London, 1948.
Pincherle, M.	*Vivaldi*, New York, 1957.

Rolland, R.	*Les Origines du Théâtre lyrique moderne*, Paris, 1931.
Sachs, C.	*The Rise of Music in the Ancient World*, New York, 1943.
Schenker, H.	*Neue Musikalische Theorien und Phantasien*, Vienna, 1906–35.
Schoenberg, A.	*Structural Functions of Harmony*, New York, 1954.
	Style and Idea, New York, 1950.
Simpson, R.	*Carl Nielsen, Symphonist*, London, 1952.
Stein, E.	*Form and Performance*, London, 1962.
Stravinsky, I.	*Chronicle of my Life*, London, 1936.
	Poétique musicale (3rd edn), Dijon, 1945.
	Conversations with Igor Stravinsky, London, 1959.
Streatfield, R. A.	*Opera*, London, 1925.
Tovey, D. F.	*A Companion to 'The Art of Fugue'*, London, 1931.
	Musical Articles from the *Encyclopedia Britannica*, London, 1944.
	Essays and Lectures on Music, London, 1949.
	Essays in Musical Analysis, London, 1935–44.
	Beethoven, London, 1944.
Toye, F.	*Verdi*, London, 1931.
Wagner, R.	*Mein Leben*, Munich, 1911.
Walker, A.	*A Study in Musical Analysis*, London, 1962.
	An Anatomy of Musical Criticism, London, 1966.
Weingartner, F.	*On the Performance of Beethoven's Symphonies*, London, 1907.
Wellesz, E.	*Essays on Opera*, London, 1950.
White, E. W.	*Stravinsky*, London, 1966.
Wishart, P.	*Harmony*, London, 1956.

Worsthorne, S. T.	*Venetian Opera in the Seventeenth Century*, Oxford, 1954.
Wyzewa, T. de / Saint-Foix, G.	*Mozart, sa vie musicale et son oeuvre*, Paris, 1937–9.
Yasser, J.	*A Theory of Evolving Tonality*, New York, 1932.
Zuckerkandl, V.	*Sound and Symbol*, New York, 1956.
	The Sense of Music, Princeton, 1959.

INDEX